647-5272

Saying Goodbye
to Daniel

Juliet Cassuto Rothman

Saying Goodbye to Daniel

When Death Is the Best Choice

CONTINUUM · NEW YORK

1995

The Continuum Publishing Company
370 Lexington Avenue
New York, NY 10017

Copyright © 1995 by Juliet Cassuto Rothman

Printed in the United States of America

Library of Congress Cataloging-in-Publication Data

Rothman, Juliet Cassuto, 1942–
    Saying goodbye to Daniel : when death is the best choice / Juliet Cassuto Rothman.
        p.   cm.
    Includes bibliographical references (pp. 168–180)
    ISBN 0-8264-0857-5 (hard : alk. paper)
    1. Rothman, Daniel Maurice, 1971–1992—Health. 2. Quadriplegics —United States—Biography. 3. Medical ethics. 4. Do-not-resuscitate orders. 5. Life support systems (Critical care) 6. Euthanasia. I. Title.
RC406.Q33R687   1995
174'.24—dc20   95-32338
                                                                      CIP

...Contents

For my family—
my husband, Leonard;
my daughters, Susan and Deborah;
and the memory
of my beloved son,
Daniel

and

For Daniel's friends and caregivers

. . . Foreword

*S*aying *Goodbye to Daniel* offers each of us a special gift: it welcomes us into the heart of Daniel and his family, so that we may walk beside them through tragedy toward an honest and courageous peace.

It has been a special privilege for me to share in the family's experience, to stand with them, and to offer them my sincere support and affection.

Little can be said to prepare the reader for this journey. All that can be asked is an open mind, a caring heart, and an understanding and accepting spirit.

—Lester Butt
Director of Psychology
Craig Hospital
Englewood, Colorado

The Accident

The phone rang at 11:30 at night, on July 3. It jangled loudly and discordantly in the carpetless beach house.

"We got a call from the police department in Rochester," our housesitter said. "They said to call right away."

I did not look at Leonard's face. I did not think.

I could hear him talking in the distance, far away. He was saying something about Daniel, our son. Something about an accident, and a broken neck, an ambulance, paramedics. He was saying that Daniel couldn't move, but he was conscious and talking. He was saying we'd be there as soon as we could.

I sat in the wooden chair opposite him. There was a terrible ringing in my ears and my head was pounding so hard that I had to hold it.

"Daniel's had a bad accident," Leonard said. "He was diving in a pool, and he broke his neck. He can't move. They think he might have injured his spinal cord."

I screamed and screamed. I could hear myself screaming from a distance, the screams echoing in my head, pounding with every heartbeat. I could not stop screaming.

This is not really me screaming, I thought. I remembered the scream of a friend's husband, when they told him his son was dead. It was that kind of scream. But my son isn't dead, I reasoned calmly, so why am I screaming like this?

"You're lying," I accused. "Why are you lying to me? You're lying. Nothing happened. It's not real and you're just lying. Why are you lying?"

"I wish I was lying, but I'm not. He's on his way to the hospital. They're taking him to Strong. He's not there yet."

"I don't believe you. You're lying," I screamed again.

Leonard was in sitting in a circle of light from the table lamp near the phone. It seemed the only light in the room. All around me was swirling darkness, the abyss, yawning open and terrifying.

"You have to believe me, Julie," he said again, "We have to go to Rochester."

"Call the hospital. Call them," I kept screaming. "They'll tell you you're lying. Why would you lie to me?" I was wailing and crying, and rocking back and forth in my chair.

After a while, he spoke to the emergency room doctors and nurses. Daniel had arrived. He was awake, conscious. The doctors told Leonard that they would try traction on his neck, because it was very far out of alignment. They did not know if it would work. He was going right in for the procedure.

I listened in silence, was suddenly galvanized into action. I wanted to be sure he was alive, sure they were not lying to me. I wanted to tell him we were coming as fast as we could. I wanted to talk to him. I took the phone from Leonard.

"Please let me talk to him," I begged.

"I'm sorry, that's just not possible. There are no phones in reach of patients in the emergency room."

"Please, I'm so far away. I'm in Rehoboth Beach, Delaware. I won't get to my son for hours. Please, please let me talk to him. Let me tell him we're coming."

"Just a minute."

The minute lasted an eternity. I clung to the phone desperately.

"Hold on, we're getting a phone to him," the nurse said.

A moment later I heard a soft "hi," and it was Daniel.

Words of comfort, relief, and strength came. I don't know how, but I was a calm, caring, loving mother, the mother Daniel had always known. He seemed so very far away, weak sounding, tired. I tried to be strong, reassuring. I told him we would come as soon as we could. Too soon, they came to take the phone away. I asked if my husband could speak.

"I messed up, Dad," Daniel told him. "I really messed up."

He hung up, and we stared at each other. We knew that we stood at the edge of a precipice, and that our lives had changed irrevocably, unalterably.

Our son, strong, active, twenty-one years old, was a student at University of Rochester. He had just completed his junior year, and was planning to apply to medical school. He had recently told us he had made dean's list, again, had completed his medical school applications, and was preparing to take the Medical College Admission Test. He had had a wonderful job monitoring patients at the Rochester Sleep Disorder Clinic during the school year—so wonderful that he had asked if he could remain in Rochester to continue it for part of the summer, and we had agreed. He and several fraternity brothers had rented a house for their senior year, and Daniel had stayed in that house, as the summer began, working at the sleep disorder clinic.

On Sunday, July 5, thirty-six hours from the time of his accident, he was to have come home, to begin a physics course at Johns Hopkins. I had his room in order, his bed made and ready for him, and his favorite food in the freezer and pantry. I was joyfully looking forward to spending a wonderful six weeks with him, before he returned to finish out the summer working in Rochester.

Friends were with us, spending the weekend that we had planned so lightheartedly several months before. They had stood by, stunned and silent, while we called. While I screamed. Now they leapt into action.

"How will you get to Rochester?"

"I don't know. With a plane."

"It's the middle of the night. Friday night. It's July Fourth weekend."

Other July Fourths swept through my mind. Images lingered briefly, faded. I could still hear my screams, echoing in my head.

"Call the airlines."

"Which ones? Where's the nearest airport?"

Focusing on the planes was concrete, easy. We all did that very well. We called US Air, Delta. We called Rehoboth Airport, Salisbury Airport, Wilmington Airport, Baltimore-Washington Airport. We called private airports to try to hire a plane. We called the police. We called local hospitals. Everywhere, we encountered dead ends. No answers. No flights.

The drive stretched ahead of us in the darkness, but we realized it was impossible. It would take us twelve hours. In our condition, it was far too many. Defeated, numb, we booked the first morning flight to Rochester. It left at 8 and arrived at 10:05.

We called our daughters in California. Neither one was home. We left messages that Daniel had been severely injured, and that we were going to Rochester. They were to wait until they heard from us.

We couldn't seem to stop calling the hospital, but there was little additional information. Eventually, they told us the traction procedure had not worked, and that Daniel would be transferred to intensive care.

At two, we left for the two-and-a-half-hour trip to the airport, leaving our friends to lock up in the morning.

The road was familiar. I knew that road from years of driving it, at all hours, in all seasons, under all conditions, but it looked unknown and strange on this night. Normalcy had fled, somewhere. Everything blurred as it went past the window and I was grateful that my husband was driving. Here and there, in the still darkness, the bare bulbs of occasional street lamps accentuated our loneliness, our horror, and our isolation. Small towns sped by, filled with people safe in their beds, sleeping peacefully.

We stopped under one of those street lamps, where a phone booth was illuminated. I was surprised that it seemed to work like a normal phone booth. I struggled with my wallet, my phone card. The nurse was not sympathetic.

"You might as well face it," she said. "Your son's a quad. He'll never walk or move again. You have to face it. He's on his way up to the ICU, the intensive care unit, now. There's nothing more to tell you. There's nothing that can be done."

I sank to the ground. The rocks around the phone booth bit into my hands as I sobbed. Leonard came to get me, and we slowly got back into the car.

"There's no sense in worrying, till we get there," he said. "We just don't know anything. We can't keep calling. No more phone booths. We just have to wait."

The unspoken words hung in the air. We'll have a lifetime to deal with this. There was nothing we could do now.

We passed near our home but couldn't face going in, though our common sense told us to get changes of clothing, shampoo, toothbrushes for the unknown time ahead. It was as though we could not bring our new reality home, not yet. We were tired and disheveled, and our beach clothes were already strangely out of place with our altered circumstances. We drove on.

From the airport, I finally called the hospital again. This time, the nurse I spoke to promised to watch over him, to take very special care of him till I got there. Vaguely reassured, I called my daughters. They had called the beach house and spoken to our friends. Susan and Debbie and Michael, Susan's husband, were all in bed together, with Daniel's pictures lined up against the headboard. They were furious that I would not let them get on a plane immediately, but I insisted that they wait until we had seen Daniel. I don't know why, but I felt we had to see him first, to prepare the girls for what they would find. I called some friends, our mothers.

Finally, it was time to board. The propeller plane flew slowly toward Rochester, as I stared numbly out of the windows at the roofs of the farmhouses of Pennsylvania, then of New York. Around us, the other passengers talked and napped and drank coffee, from that other world we no longer lived in. How often had I taken Daniel to this plane, during the three years that he had been a student at the University of Rochester?

The massive blocks of buildings that were Strong Memorial Hospital appeared, too soon. Now that I was finally here, I realized that I was frightened. I didn't want to know. It was easier, in a way, to be in ignorance.

As we walked down the hall of the ICU that first morning, I stopped Leonard and took him by the arm.

"From this moment on," I said seriously, "we will never look back. We will look only forward, and build a new world for Daniel. It will do no good to look back. We can only go ahead."

He nodded in silence, and in silence we moved on.

At the desk in the ICU, they were waiting for us.

"Before you go in, we have to talk," said someone in a white coat, a doctor. We obediently followed him to his office. I was terrified. Now they will tell us, I thought, that he is really dead. That's why they won't let us see him.

"We have Daniel scheduled for surgery. We waited until you got here, but we have no time. He must go in ten minutes. The OR is ready. He has to have reduction surgery to try to realign his neck bones. He has a C4 fracture. There are no choices. He must have the surgery."

The surgeon popped his head in the door.

"There's a one-in-a-thousand chance that the surgery will enable him to regain his function," he said. "We must do it to stabilize his neck. We have to do it right away. We can't wait any longer."

One in a thousand. How do you like them odds, baby?, I thought to myself. That's like—no chance. But then, we've always been lucky. Maybe we'll be the ones.

"And by the way," he said casually, almost as an afterthought, "we have to intubate him. We have to go too near the phrenic nerve, which controls breathing. It's just a precautionary measure. It will come out after surgery, with no problem."

We agreed to the surgery. We were numb, in shock, beyond thought or understanding. I would have agreed to anything, at that moment, just to be allowed to see my son.

I will never forget that first moment. Daniel was in what is called a halo—a black headband that looks like its namesake. It has horrible screws that protrude, and press against the skull. He had IVs dripping, and he was, of course, motionless. I barely noticed all the machines and tubing. I could take in only his face, and that face was still the face of my son—my Daniel, still with his sparkle in his eyes, his ready smile. He could speak, and he was aware and alert.

I did not cry. I just held on to him. I was happy to just be with him, and so in shock from what I saw and was being asked to absorb and accept that I was beyond tears. I was so grateful to find him alive.

Too few minutes, and the aides took him away to surgery. We had lost so much, but we did not know how much more we were losing, in that very moment, and in those hours that followed.

Daniel was in surgery for five hours. When the doctor finally came to tell us it was done, he was very pleased with himself. He said he had heard Daniel's bones "snap back into place." Daniel was on his way back to the ICU.

We went back upstairs, back to Daniel. He was asleep, but he looked awful. He had a tube down his throat, more IVs, his halo. I became aware for the first time of all the monitors clicking away. I stood and watched him for as long as they let me.

The kids that had saved him, that had leapt into the pool seconds after he had, and that had enabled him to be conscious and alive, came by to see us. I was so grateful to see them that the tears flowed, for the first time since I had seen Daniel. I hugged each of them tightly. Their bodies felt so warm and healthy. Can it be, I thought, that Daniel's isn't like this anymore? That it never will be like this again?

Later, Susan and Debbie arrived, each carrying her favorite teddy bear in her arms, each in blue jeans and a shirt, looking lost and scared and vulnerable. My babies, I thought. Twenty-five and twenty-four, carrying their teddies to comfort them from the horror of the unknown they were about to face.

Carrying them all the way on that long flight from California. My maternal protective urges wanted to shield them from the sight of Daniel, but there was no shielding possible. Holding their teddies, they went in to their brother.

We were all together, finally. Somehow, we would all come through this, I was sure. All together, as always. Ours was a family that always faced things together. We would face this.

The thought comforted me.

. . .2

The Hospital

It was several days before I became aware of my new surroundings, before things stopped being a blur, before I could clearly see anything beyond Daniel's face. Slowly, bits and pieces of my new world came into focus.

The intensive care unit was on the eighth floor of Strong Memorial, a large university teaching hospital. As my awareness grew, one of the first things I noticed was that it was badly in need of refurbishing. Its old dark wood doors and trim were covered with deep gashes and scratches, the marks of beds, x-ray machines, oxygen carts, and unknown other pieces of equipment pushed against them in the rush to save a life. The walls were beige and dirty and bare, and the dinginess made a terribly depressing situation drearier than ever. Rows of extra beds and equipment lined the halls. There was little privacy.

The ICU waiting room was so crowded much of the time that people sat on the floor in the hall. It was a room with bare beige walls and dark green carpeting, forever dirty from the unending stream of visitors. The seats were green plastic, single and double, with wooden arms. It was impossible to get comfortable in them. There was a round table with four side chairs, a coffee table, a old, battered desk of unknown purpose, with no accompanying chair. There were soda machines and snack machines. There were two pay phones on the wall. The uncurtained window stretched the length of the room.

There were two small waiting rooms, one off the main waiting room, and another that opened onto the hall, so small that with the door closed one immediately became unable to breathe. I called the small room off the waiting room "the death room," convinced from the beginning that this is where they took people to tell them that their loved one had died. I refused to ever go there, though everyone repeatedly told me this was not so. Later, many times, I heard the screams and sobs that came from that room, the priest or minister or rabbi go in and come out.

Daniel had been admitted to the hospital through the emergency room. He was a student at the hospital's university, had for the past year been a volunteer at that hospital, was the child of a physician. He had full insurance coverage. He had been assigned to a surgeon for his neck surgery, who was sympathetic, but who left shortly after the surgery for vacation and was gone until two or three days before we ourselves left Strong. He had no attending physician who was in overall charge of his care. We, his parents, in shock and desperate, were not aware that we could have requested a personal physician. Sophisticated as we were about the medical establishment, the terrible events had numbed us and had taken our normal reasoning faculties. We felt helpless to protest, helpless to demand.

Over the course of the four weeks that we were to remain at Strong Memorial, many specialists were called to work with Daniel. Without exception, they would not speak with me. The technology and equipment was the best possible; the medical care, utterly impersonal.

On the third or fourth day, a young doctor came toward me.

"You don't seem to have anyone coordinating Daniel's care," he said, "and I know you're worried. Will you accept me for now as his primary care physician? I am a fellow in intensive care."

I was so grateful, I began to cry. Dr. K. was young, and did not have the years of experience that Daniel's condition might have warranted. But he cared. And he made a medical situation which was the stuff of hate articles against the medical establishment livable and bearable for Daniel and for his family. We met with him daily to discuss the events of the past twenty-four hours and the plans for the next. He was always there when we needed him. And we needed him often.

In marked contrast to the physicians, the ICU nurses were outstanding. The nurses provided all of Daniel's care, and watched over him carefully. He often had one-on-one care—one nurse just for him: her (or his) only job was Daniel. Without these very special people, Daniel's life would have been shorter, more painful, more bitter. They loved him and hugged him and babied him and coddled him and spoke to him seriously and advocated for him. They pushed themselves to the utmost and took on incredible responsibility to try to make his life a bit more bearable. They came to visit him on their days off, requested to care for him, and came to say "hi" even when they were not scheduled to work with him.

One nurse's story stands out in my mind as very special. Nurse Nancy had taken care of Daniel for several days and had become very fond of him. She was caring for her other patient when she heard Daniel's "nurse noise"—the only sound he could make, from across the room. She looked at the monitors and saw his pulse dropping to zero. She dropped what she was doing and rushed to him to find that his ventilator tubing had disconnected, and he had gone into cardiac arrest. She acted quickly, and Daniel revived. Later, desperate, almost in tears, she told me that she had failed. In that moment when she was alone with him and he was recording no pulse, she had gotten upset. Tears had clouded her vision, emotion her decisions. She judged herself to be a failure as a nurse, for she had not kept her distance. I judged her a success. She had cared.

When Daniel had arrived in the ICU, he had been placed in a "pod"—a room with five or six beds and all the support equipment needed by each, separated by glass and wood partitions that extended halfway down the length of each bed. There was very little room: barely enough for the caregivers, none for family. There was no privacy, and no way to linger. I wanted to be able to stay more than the allotted minutes, and this was very difficult. However, the nurses accomodated me, even setting up a "cardiac chair" by Daniel's bed for me to sleep in when I needed to be with him.

As I went down the hall toward Daniel from my third weary night in the ICU waiting room, I found him in transit. Daniel was being moved to a room I had not known could exist in Strong's old and battered ICU—a private room with four walls, a large window with a view, a toilet (which he never used), and space for family seating and visiting. This room was a special gift from the nurses—they wanted Daniel and his family to be comfortable. And, insofar as possible under the terrible circumstances in which we found ourselves, we were.

Toward the end of our time at Strong, I became obsessed with the need for Daniel to see the outside world, to leave his ICU room cocoon and see that the world was still there, the world to which I somehow still hoped that he would return. Taking a patient on a ventilator out of the ICU, downstairs and outdoors was an unheard of proposition, a mammouth task involving the willingness to take on enormous responsibility. And yet, twice, Daniel went outdoors. The first time, we took him right in his bed with the portable vent on a cart and his IV poles swinging bags of IV fluid. It was raining and Daniel could smell the trees and the grass and watch people come and go. He took it all in in huge eyefuls, grateful for the change of scene and a brief contact with some kind of normalcy. This twenty-minute interlude involved Dr. K., Daniel's nurse, and his respiratory technician. We were a parade of five for one patient. But each felt a sense of exhilaration and wonder at our astonishing achievment!

A few days later Daniel wanted to go out again. He had a male nurse who decided he could handle this all himself. Daniel was placed on a portable ventilator, the ventilator balanced on his bed, emergency oxygen set between his legs to keep it steady, IV's connected to the bed itself, and away we went, out the side door, into a beautiful sunny day. The nurse wheeled Daniel up and away from the hospital in his big heavy bed, and finally parked him under a tree. He had even brought sunglasses, for Daniel's eyes were unprotected in his prone position!

I do not remember much else of the hospital. Sometimes I went to the cafeteria with Susan and Debbie for lunch. The cashier lady became my friend. The cafeteria was a gloomy affair in dark red, with big windows. I sat at the windows and looked out at the world and remembered, idly, that I used to belong to that world. People walked by, laughing and talking. Cars came and went. The sky was sometimes gray, sometimes blue. Sometimes it was night and the street lights made glowing shadows of the cars as they passed. I saw that the world was still the same, out there. But I didn't belong to it any more.

...3

My Son Is a Quad

I knew very little—nothing really, about this condition, quadriplegia, that my son now had. I had worked with a quad, once, a patient in a nursing home where I was the consulting social worker. I remembered that he was a C6 level. I had no idea what that meant. My nursing home patient was angry, and frustrated. Daily, he looked down the hall at the moaning, confused, wandering elderly, helpless. Daniel could not be like that, I thought. I will not let him. Yet, what could I do to stop it?

One thing I remembered: the importance of keeping muscles and joints moving well in case any function returned. During the first day or two, this was my focus: getting Daniel some range of motion. My daughters and I worked with him frequently. We moved his fingers and hands, his arms, his legs. Finally, I was able to have physical therapy ordered. The therapist came daily, doing range of motion exercises with Daniel and instructing us, at my request, in the correct techniques. In a world where we felt so helpless to do anything useful, keeping Daniel's limbs flexible was a concrete task that comforted us all.

The other thing that I remembered was that Daniel would need extensive rehabilitation, and that hospitals differed greatly in the kind and extent of rehabilitation they offered. I asked Strong's rehabilitation department for information and they gave me several suggestions: Craig Hospital, in Denver, if I wanted the very best; National Rehabilitation Hospital, in Washington, if I wanted Daniel nearby; and Allied Rehabilitation, in Pennsylvania, were among them. Immediately, I called each for information.

I hungered for knowledge about quadriplegia. I felt lost and adrift in a world that kept shifting around, far away from how it used to be. I was left stranded in new and unfamiliar places. I knew too little to guide the shifts, or even prepare myself and Daniel for them. Using all of the hospital's information resources, I began the desperate search for information. I called hotlines and information numbers, visited rehabilitation centers, and talked with healthcare personnel who dealt with quadriplegics.

Still, there were so many questions that I felt only others in our situation could answer: how were they managing? What about school, jobs, marriage, children? From various sources, people with answers came, each one more giving and helpful than the last. I spoke to parents of quadriplegics, spouses, children, and patients themselves. I spoke to them about their rehabilitation experiences, their equipment needs, and how they managed their lives. I spoke to a college student in the Rochester area several times. He was very helpful. Learning how he had organized his life and education was inspiring. Since I would not leave the hospital, these people came there to talk with me.

I called the University of Rochester, to let them know what had happened, and to find out what they would be able to do to help Daniel finish school. He kept saying he wanted to return to school, under any circumstances. The school was very supportive, and the dean of students came to visit Daniel several times. The academic dean's office assisted me by arranging for Daniel to do a "course" while he was in rehabilitation, and by assuring me that dormitory accomodations would and could be modified to meet Daniel's new needs. Daniel was pleased with all of this, but wanted more. He wanted the senior year he had planned on, worked so hard to achieve. He wanted to go back to the house he had rented for the year with four other friends, and to eat his meals in the fraternity house.

More calls, more arrangements. Daniel could share an accessible room in the home that he had rented with his best friend from school. His fraternity, Theta Chi, would undertake modifications to the house that would permit Daniel access to meals at the house, meetings, parties, and so on. Fraternity brothers offered to take Daniel to classes, even to go to classes with him, to help him. They offered to take notes, sit by him, and give all the assistance he needed.

Meanwhile, information about spinal cord injury started arriving. I read and read and read, until I felt satisfied that I knew what I needed to know. I talked with Daniel frequently about what I was learning. Yes, it might be possible to have children. Yes, he could operate a computer. There were wonderful community resources. He would be taught how to handle and direct the help that would be needed daily. He could make it on his own, if he wished, away from us. We were not afraid to let him, and he was not afraid to go.

We discussed what I had learned about research, work that was being done with nerves and with the spinal cord, in Miami and in other areas of the country. We thought that, perhaps, research would bring help in Daniel's lifetime, that this would not go on forever, though breakthroughs did not seem too imminent.

I felt strong, capable of dealing with this. I felt optimistic that, somehow, things would work out, and that Daniel would finish school. I even believed that, somehow, he would still go to medical school as he planned. Hadn't he filled out the applications, gotten the references, written the essays? Hadn't they just passed the Americans with Disabilities Act? Of course, he would go. He would just have to have someone help him with "hands on" learning. Daniel kept saying he "hoped so." He wanted very much to go. He had worked so hard, for so many years, for the future that he had envisioned. With all my strength and will and ability, I wanted to help him to make this possible. And, those first days and weeks, I was sure that, together, we could achieve anything.

I had also learned the tremendous difference that the most minute change in level could make. Daniel was a C4–5 on admission. That meant that he would not have the use of his arms or his hands, but would have some use of his shoulders. A C5–6 quadriplegic had a great deal more independence. I kept hoping that a miracle would happen. Just one little level, I prayed. One fraction of an inch. The possibility of the reverse, a *loss* in levels, did not occur to me. Though Daniel had, in fact, lost all of C4, and C3 as well, after his surgery, I did not worry, secure in the explanations I was given. It was swelling, I was told. It will go away.

What neither Daniel nor I understood, in those beginning days, was that his body would not cooperate. It listened to us, it tried, but it could not assist us with our plans.

Daniel could not seem to get back off the ventilator and breathe on his own, as he had before his surgery. Eventually, he had a tracheotomy to make breathing easier. He could not move at all, even his head. He could only move his eyes and mouth words. Of course, he could not eat or drink, and a naso-gastric tube was inserted so that he could receive some nutrition. Patiently, and with perfect faith, we believed what we were told: he would get off the ventilator and return to his admission level of functioning C4–5.

On the third day, Susan brought a slice of pizza to me as I sat by Daniel's bed, as ususal. I took a bite, turned to Daniel, and something terrible happened. Bells went off and lights flashed. Nurses ran over, pushing me aside. I was quickly escorted to the hall, my heart pounding, terrified. Daniel had had his first loss in pulse and blood pressure, his first cardiac arrest.

As soon as they let me, I went back to the room and gripped the railing of his bed and cried. They could not release my grip for a long time. I was afraid to leave, and the nurses let me stay in a chair by Daniel, so I could watch him. I was terrified. No one had told me about this, and nothing I had read had prepared me.

Daniel was apparently one of the rare quadriplegics who had this problem, which supposedly occurred from the fourth to the fourteenth day only. Some quadriplegics died at this point: they could not be resuscitated.

Die? I thought. Not possible. I must stay with him. I must guard him.

I guarded.

I asked Dr. K. what else could go wrong. I don't remember the answers I was given. They had to do with kidney infections, pneumonia, blood problems. Nothing sank in, because the terror of the cardiac arrests overrode everything else.

In spite of all of these new and terrible medical events, I knew that I was going to get Daniel through this. Hadn't I gotten him through all kinds of other things throughout his life? Hadn't I dealt with football injuries, high school pranks, childhood illnesses, friendship crises? Didn't I know my own child: how he thought, how he reacted to things, what he believed spiritually? Didn't I know his values? Hadn't I, in fact, helped him to develop them? I knew he could "hang in there" and ride out the storm. He always had. I knew he had strength of will and a determination to achieve whatever he chose to achieve. I knew that he would have a terrible time adjusting to his physical limitations, but I also knew that he would be able to do this, and emerge from his new condition stronger and even more special a person than he already was. I knew that my job, as his mother, was to be there, to support him, and to help him to define his new self, his new world. I knew that Daniel would do something very special in life, even more special, though perhaps different, now. The young man who wanted "to bring quality medical care to underdeveloped countries" might need to find something a bit different to do, now. But do something special, meaningful, worthwhile? I knew he would.

My son was a quadreplegic. I understood better, now, what that word meant. Yet, I saw in this opportunities for growth for him, and for us, his parents and sisters. We would accept what there was, and move on from there.

We had some very hard times, of course. Daniel and I talked about this too, he mouthing his words patiently. We decided that I would keep a daily journal of these first weeks, that everyone said were the hardest. When Daniel was back in the world, we would write my notes into a book for new quadreplegics and their families, to help them cope, and to give them the information and hope that they needed. We were going to turn these difficult times into something good and useful for others. Write a book, finish school, and go on to graduate school. These were not only possibilities, they were certainties. With enthusiasm, I went to the gift shop, bought a notebook, and began our history.

4

In the Hours of Darkness

Though we had all stayed in the hospital the first two nights, when Leonard left to try to adapt his professional life to his new circumstances, I moved into the hospital more permanently. My son needed me, right nearby, for he was helpless. I, his mother, and his sisters with me, became homeless persons. It was necessary. There was so much to learn, so much to do, so much need to be right there.

During that first week, we were alone every night in the ICU waiting room. We waited patiently, and, by around eleven, all of the visitors had left. The nurses gave us pillows and blankets. We pulled the couches together to form a private "home." We spread our blankets on them. We snacked from our "kitchen," the pile of food and drink supplies that friends of Daniel's and Susan's in-laws kept stocked for us in a corner by the window. We lay our faces down on the hard seats that were too short for a body to lie on. We pulled the blankets over our heads, exhausted beyond imagining, and went to sleep.

Countless times, I would wake and go down the hall to see Daniel, to be sure he was alive. His body, warm and tanned and strong, with muscles filled out and bulging, reassured me. Nothing could happen to that body, I thought. Not really. I would watch him a while in silence, and then slowly walk back to my "home."

Countless times, during those long nights, someone would come in for a soda. The "clunck" would wake us all up, each time. Wearily, we would look up, and then lie back down. Sometimes, someone would come in and turn on some of the lights, and sit down and read. Dawn would come to the uncurtained windows, all to soon.

Around seven or eight in the morning, people would begin to arrive. We would get up, have some juice from our stores, and pile our belongings in a corner. All day, people would come and tear apart our "walls," rearranging our space to meet their immediate needs. They sat where we put our faces, on our "beds." They left soda cans and food containers on our tables. They spread newspapers everywhere. The "home" we had made was no more. This was public domain, anyone's to use and to hold.

Often, there would be no place for us in the waiting room, and we would be banished to the hall, our "home" a vague abstract concept in our minds only. But then, surely, night would come, and everyone would go home, and once again the ICU waiting room became "home." Once again we built our walls, went to our corner and took our blankets and pillows, and made our little world. And so on, as day moved through night, and on to day again.

Hours in the semi-dark, together. Hours of remembering the past, of worrying about the present, of wondering about the future. My daughters and I drifted, at sea, random thoughts flowing from each of us, bouncing against each other. In those dark hours before weary dawns, we finally shared the incredible premonitions that had clouded the days and weeks before Daniel's accident. Deeply felt, unshared, secretly kept and worried over endlessly, the premonitions finally found voice, were shared, and understood, in the context of the awsome events which surrounded us.

I begin with mine, for I know them best. Last spring, a year ago as I write this, Daniel was with us. Now, I look out of my window, at the greenness of the new grass, at the gently swaying branches, at the ripples of the creek below. The sun bounces off my neighbor's flag, off the masts of the sailboats in the distance.

My sadness mutes the colors, overshadowing each brightness with the gray of my sorrow.

Last year, at this time, I watched spring come, carefree, for the last time. I knew, for certain, that it was the last time. There was a tender bittersweetness within me as I looked out this same window, for, inside me, a voice was saying, regretfully but very, very, surely, "look, enjoy, savor. Take time to see the flowers and feel the spring breezes. Sit outside and feel the sunshine, for it is the last time. The last free, beautiful, joyous spring. The last time to see colors in all their brightness, to feel that all is right with the world. The world will change soon, and all this beauty will still be here, but you will not feel it in the same way. You will no longer be a part of it."

I listened to the voice. I took special time. I sat in the sun, dangled my feet by the water's edge. I watched the birds, touched the petals of the flowers. I searched the blue of the sky for patterns, patterns of my life to come. I said goodbye, slowly, with love, to all these wonders of Nature that were so very dear to me. I knew, then.

And, in May, the images started. Terrible, dreadful images, so clear and so repetitive that I could not ignore them. I saw a child's face down in the water, at the bottom of a pool. The face was still, unmoving. A leaf floated lazily on the surface. The water was clear and I gazed down in horror at—my daughter's face. Susan's face.

Terror gripped me, too great for words. Again and again, the image came, clear, unrelenting. Too terrified to share it with anyone, I would call Susan repeatedly.

"Watch out, Susan," I would say, afraid to tell the truth: "Be careful driving. You could have an accident. Don't go to places that are not safe. Stay home at night."

"Oh mom, I'm fine. I don't do anything stupid. You can trust me," she would say.

But I didn't believe her.

After a while, the repetition of the images became so terrifying that I told Leonard. Finally, they faded, leaving me apprehensive, and waiting, always waiting, for that inevitable phone call that finally came.

Why the wrong child? I wondered in agony after Daniel's accident. If I had had the right child, maybe I could have warned him. Why, oh why, did I get it wrong? For days, sitting by his bedside, I was tortured by this question, until the needs of the moment blocked out my speculation and not until now does it resurface. Why the wrong child?

Three days before Daniel's accident, I became severely anxious. I was at work. I began to cry, and to tell coworkers that something awful, terrible, horrible was going to happen and that my whole life would change. They tried to comfort me, but couldn't. I called Leonard at his office, crying, sobbing out my fears and terrors. He, too, could not reassure me, and, after a time, I remember feeling resigned that what would be, would be.

Debbie's story, strangely, formed the other half of mine. She had had the same dream, over and over. Susan was running across a deck. She leapt off the edge, did a flip in the air, landed on the ground, and lay still. She never moved. Debbie was terrified, much too terrified to tell anyone. Joining her story mine, we have the entire actual sequence of Daniel's accident.

Though Debbie's image, like mine, was of Susan, she had strong feelings that something was going to happen to Daniel all spring. She kept waiting for the phone call, sure that it would come. Debbie and her roomate had planned a trip to Palm Springs for the July Fourth weekend. Debbie became more and more apprehensive as the time to leave approached. She knew, somehow, that it would be this weekend that the call would come. That Friday morning, July 3, she deliberately stayed in her room, feigning sleep, until is was too late to leave. The trip was cancelled. She was relieved that she could remain at home. She had to be there, waiting for the call. Of course, the call came.

Susan had planned a trip to San Fransisco, and up into the mountains, rafting, for the July Fourth weekend. She had paid for the rafting trip, a non-refundable $400. She had her plane tickets, the car had been rented. On the same day that I was having my anxiety attack at work, she began to get strong feelings that she could not go on the trip: she had to remain at home in Los Angeles, because she was going to be needed. She called the rafting company, and asked for an exception to the no-refund policy. They said no. Susan became hysterical on the phone. She told them that there had been a terrible accident back East, and she had to fly there. She needed the money for plane fare. She said that, as she told the story, she had complete conviction of its truth. She felt desperate. The company refunded her the money. She stayed at home, waiting for the call. It came.

And I remembered Daniel's words, this spring, "Mom, I decided I'm not going to kill myself for grades. If I really kill myself, I'll only raise my grade a tiny fraction of a percentage point. It's not going to make any difference in my GPA. This may be the last spring that I can have any enjoyment, any fun. I want to have all the fun I can."

I was furious.

"Daniel," I almost shouted, "you can't do that to us. We are paying a fortune for you to be at U. of R. You have to study and get the best grades that you can. If you don't want to work your hardest, you shouldn't stay there. Come home and commute if you want to fool around."

"I'm not fooling around," he said heatedly. "I'm studying. I'll make the dean's list. I just mean I'm not going to give up all fun altogether. I want to have fun. I may never have a chance again."

He stuck to his plan. He studied, but he had fun. He made the dean's ist. It was his last time for either—fun or dean's list.

Sitting in the dark, with the glow of the soda machines casting eerie colors around the ICU waiting room, these stories seemed to bring us, and the whirlwind in which we were now caught, even closer together. In some strange, unearthly way, each of us had been prepared. We each knew that something would happen to change our lives forever. That it did, in the silence of that moment, seemed plausible and right.

At least there was some sense of continuity. It made the break between past and present less complete. It gave us reassurance that somewhere, somehow, there could still be an order and purpose to the Universe. We no longer had a firm hold on what that order and purpose was, but the stories linked us, in that place and time, to some eternal state of being that, we were all sure, trascended our lives, and the reality of the tragedy that was now ours.

The next day Daniel, struggling in pain, listened to the stories of our night. He did not relate to them. They were not where he was, then.

5

Settling In

In the beginning, I was afraid to leave the eighth floor. I needed to be where Daniel was, all the time. I slept with my daughters in the waiting room, I ate what people brought—when I could. I showered through the kindness of the staff in the on-call room. I used the staff bathroom to wash up. Always fastidious about personal hygiene, I washed my clothes in the bathroom, and put them back on my body, wet, to dry. I had no others. I had no place to be, no place to go, nothing to do, but to stay with my son. He filled my whole world, my whole consciousness. I loved him so.

After a while, I began to have a little more trust. I went for brief periods, to the cafeteria and to the gift shop for something to read. Once, I even went outside to sit on a bench for a few minutes. I never left for long. I needed to be with Daniel perhaps even more than he needed me to be there. I needed to be sure that he was OK. By which, at that time, I meant I needed to be sure that he was alive.

The moment Daniel finally told me that he was sick and tired of seeing me in in the same clothes day after day made me feel exultant. He cared, I thought triumphantly. Not about me—I knew that already—I was excited that he still cared about *appearances*. He cared how I looked to his friends, to the nurses, to *him*. I felt that was a positive sign, and happily agreed to remedy the situation.

Leaving Susan and Debbie in charge, with firm strictures not to leave him for a minute, I went with Susan's mother-in-law to the local shopping center. I needed some new clothes. These were going to be, I thought, new clothes for my new life. They would begin my life as the mother of a quad. They needed to be cheerful, pretty, practical.

"New clothes for my new life," I whispered to myself as I searched through the racks. "I'm going to have a new life, and I have to get ready for it!"

I needed everything, of course, from the skin out. I quickly chose three or four changes of clothes that I thought Daniel would like.

I returned to the hospital to find that arrangements for housing were being made. I had lived at the hospital long enough, the staff felt. I needed a bed and a shower of my own, normal food, and some time to myself. The staff suggested the Ronald McDonald House. It would be easy to arrange: I had Daniel's car to drive. It was only a few blocks away, and I could come and go when and how I pleased. Bowing to the inevitable, I agreed.

At about midnight that night, the girls and I moved into the Ronald McDonald House of Rochester, the most wonderful home away from home one could ever have. Never in my life would I have imagined what such a home can do for a family in distress, such as ours. Never in my life will I forget the wonderful people who watched over each of us, cared and shared and worried with us, and gave us, truly, a home.

Something happened inside me with the move to the Ronald McDonald House. The change in our lives assumed a kind of permanence and reality it did not have as long as we were homeless people in the ICU waiting room. For the forseeable future, this would be my home. My clothes, personal items, and mail would all be here. I could stay as long as was needed. Moving in involved hanging my few purchases, tags still dangling, in the closet area. I rarely thought of my home in Annapolis. I was, fully and completely, in Rochester.

The Ronald McDonald House had a private room and a bathroom for us. We all shared common living spaces: the living room, library, laundry, kitchen, and dining room. The kitchen had refrigerator space for each family, and a pantry with an area designated for each as well. There was also always a plentiful supply of food for anyone who needed it: bakery goods, cereal, canned goods, and other items. There was hot coffee and tea twenty-four hours a day.

Special friends sent us fruit of our own, but otherwise we snacked from the general supply. I was too tired to deal with a grocery store and could not leave the hospital long enough to shop.

I rarely saw any of the other families, for I seemed to live on a schedule all my own, out of step with the rest of the house. I came home much too late to see anyone, and often left much too early. I was always in a hurry to get to Daniel in the morning, and not of a mind to visit with others. However, at times I did see other families, other children. Each family seemed to find comfort and sustenance at the House, and each, in their own way, made it home. Each family was dealing with tragedy with all of the strength and coping skills it could muster.

Sometimes my social-worker self would assert itself, laboriously, from a distance, and I would become involved with particular problems. It felt good to be helpful, to use professional skills, to give of myself and to realize that, in spite of my own terrible problems, I still had something to give.

The director of the House was a special person. Through my darkest moments, she was there. When I returned, alone and exhausted, after a night of guarding Daniel from the Angel of Death, she was there. When I gave up hope, and was desperate, she was there. When the car battery died, she was there, with her car, to help us, nearly killing us all by connecting the wrong points on the battery charger.

Over the next days and weeks, a routine developed. I got up, had breakfast from the kitchen's supplies, drove to the hospital and moved in for the day. At midnight, I drove home, had a snack from the kitchen, and went to sleep. Sometimes I noticed that the sun was shining, briefly. Sometimes I looked quickly up at the stars. I did not think. My entire being was taken up with Daniel. There was no space for anything else.

Leonard had gone back home after two days. This had been very hard for me, but the reasons that pulled him back seemed right. He was concerned about his patients and his responsibilities to them and to his department (he was chief of Obstetrics and Gynecology); and he felt that Daniel would need huge financial resources for an optimal quality of life, which he had to earn to provide. He commuted back and forth, visiting us for weekends. Debbie stayed two weeks, and went back to work at her law clerk job. Susan, still in her first year of marriage, stayed two and a half weeks and returned home. Each came often over the course of the summer, and stayed as long as they could.

Only I stayed all the time and never left. In the ten and a half weeks of Daniel's life after his accident, I left him once, for three days, and once, for a scant two. Otherwise, I was with him every day, and many, many, nights, as well. There was nothing that could be more important, in my life, than to be with him. I was grateful to all of my jobs, for their understanding and helpfulness. I left my summer teaching job two weeks into the summer semester, and had to cancel my fall classes. I left two nursing homes uncovered, with no licensed social worker for two and a half months. I left my husband's office with no administrative assistant, left all my volunteer positions, all my responsibilities at home.

I am so glad that I did this: glad that I took the time to spend what was to be Daniel's last summer with him. Each day, each conversation was precious, and renewed the strength and beauty of our relationship—both Daniel's and mine, and ours as a family. I can never have Daniel back, I know. But the precious time that we shared that last summer had a beauty for me greater than the greatest works of art, the most moving music. They were *our* art, *our* music.

... 6

Of Heart Lines and Phone Lines

As Daniel and I attempted to begin to grapple with our completely new life circumstances, each of us turned first to the other for help.

I wanted very much to try to understand how Daniel felt, how he understood and interpreted the world with his altered senses and mobility. I spent countless hours just imagining. I tried to be very still, to immobilize myself, remaining that way for periods of time. But, it seemed to me that, try as I might, with all my heart and will and soul, I could not sense the world as Daniel did. I could always feel the coolness of the air, the binding of my belt or shoes, the touch of my blouse against my skin. I would invariably begin to develop an itch, and end up abandoning the enterprise to scratch. Trying to resist did help me to understand a little of Daniel's agony. Lying still in bed, unable to move, his nose would itch, or his eye need to be rubbed. Each time, he had to ask for help. If he got feverish, and sweaty, someone had to wipe his brow.

"How does it feel?" I would ask him in desperation, out of my need to understand. "I try to imagine, but I can't."

"It doesn't feel like anything. Just my head always feels hot, and I itch, and my head hurts. Mostly I just feel uncomfortable," he would mouth at me.

"Can you feel here," I would ask hopefully, touching his shoulder.

"No," he would answer. "I can't feel anything except my face. And it feels so uncomfortable."

"Do you feel your insides?"

"I think so. Sometimes it feels like I have a stomach ache. And it hurts when they suction me, inside my chest. Sometimes it feels like I have to go to the bathroom. I tell the nurse, but I'm always wrong, and I don't have to."

"Do you want to watch TV? Can I read to you?"

Mostly, the answer was no. He just wanted to think, he said, immersed in the tragedy and the attempt to understand his body.

After a week or two, I began more insistent.

"Just because you can't move doesn't mean you have to just lie here and stare at the ceiling," I pleaded. "We could read, or at least, watch TV. I'm tired of sitting and staring."

And so, we worked out a plan. He "thought" and slept all day. In the evening, we raised his head for about an hour or two, and watched the summer Olympics. It was all he wanted to see. It broke my heart to watch the beautiful athletes, bodies and muscles toned to the utmost, to watch them swim, and run, and dive, and jump, and know that Daniel would never, never, never do any of those things again. I thought it would make him sad to watch, but he kept saying he was interested.

It seemed to be all he was interested in. Our days were measured by Olympic events, by medals forever out of reach. An unbridgeable distance there was, between the starry-eyed athlete on the stand, listening to the National Anthem, and Daniel and I, sitting quietly in the ICU, with the machines whirring and clicking around us. And yet, watching in silence, there was a measure of peace.

Sometimes Daniel would let me sing to him before he went to sleep. I sang him songs from his childhood, songs from long trips in the car in the dark, songs he had loved when he was young, and songs he had hated, teasing him until he smiled at me in spite of himself. The one he hated the most was "Leaving on a Jet Plane." His favorites were "Country Roads," and "There's a Land That I See."

Sometimes he let me read to him. He loved the Greek myths, and poetry, and short stories. Then, I would tuck him in, turn out the lights, call for his sleeping medicine, and sit and watch the monitors in the dark. Many times I stayed all night, sensing that my presence brought comfort and security, and that, if he needed anything, Mom was best to provide it. I sat in a chair, with a pillow and a sheet, and tried to sleep while at the same time watch and listen. It seemed to me I was asleep and awake at the same time.

I had recently taken a course in guided imagery, and I used this with Daniel also. I stood for long periods at his bedside, speaking quietly and calmly, giving him images that were peaceful and enjoyable to him, always staying within the parameters of what he could experience as a quadriplegic. Sometimes I gave him memories of things we had done, places we had seen. But always, I gave him images in which he could function as he was. Imagery calmed him when he was agitated, eased him when he was upset or depressed, helped him to sleep at night. Imagery helped us both to envision a future, and to remember a past. They took us far from the hospital, far from the sounds of the ventilator and the monitors and the dripping of the IVs. Sometimes I played music while I spoke, the soft sounds silencing the noises outside our room, isolating us in a world of harmony and peace.

After the first week or so I could feel the bond between us grow and strengthen. After all, we were together each and every day. Daniel and I had always had a very close and spiritual relationship. We had always talked over everything in his life, and everything in mine. We shared our views of the world, and of everything and everyone in it. This we had always done. But, with the accident and his new limitations, and new respect and intimacy developed. I tried to keep him interested, motivated in living. I listened to and honored all of his choices and wishes that were within my power to act upon. I treated his dependency lightly and casually so that he never felt he was a burden to me. I talked about staying in Rochester and getting used to a new city, a change of scene, though in truth I never saw anything outside of the hospital. He tried to be cheerful, at least part of the time.

When Leonard and Susan and Debbie were all gone, I had a moment of loneliness. I shared it with Daniel.

"I feel so alone," I told him sadly. "Everybody's gone. I'm here all by myself. Sometimes it's hard."

"I know," Daniel mouthed sympathetically. "But, Mom, you aren't really alone, you know. I'm here."

That's true," I said and started to cry, "How could I not have thought of that. Daniel, you'll still have to take care of me. I'll take care of you and you'll take care of me."

He made a face. "If you want me to take care of you, you'll have to mostly stay in this room."

"I will," I promised. "After all, I have to take care of you, too, and this is where you are."

And so, the agreement was made. And, in his special way, Daniel *did* take care of me. All the way to the end, and through it, he took care of me. In a special sense, he still does, and always will.

But then, there was always the hope that things would improve. I spoke of the future as though thinking would make it so. I believed in it with all my strength. I believed that Daniel would have a meaningful life, would be able to accomplish his life goals.

He would listen carefully, "I hope so," he would say. "I want to finish school. I want to go to medical school. I really do hope I can."

"You can," I said. "Everything is all arranged. And if you decide you can't, or don't want to, we'll find something else you will like."

Always, I was careful to give choices: "You can come back to college, if you want to, as soon as you finish rehab. Or, you can come home to us for a while. You know I'd *love* to spend time with you. If you want, you can go to University of Maryland. I can take you. It's no problem. There are lots of things you can do, lots of choices you can make. You don't have to decide anything now. I just want you to know that we will help you to have whatever life you want, wherever you want."

Daniel would look at me sadly, "I know, Mom. I know you will. We'll just have to see. I don't know what I'll do without my hands."

Part of our daily ritual was doing "exercises," and providing special skin care. In the first weeks, Daniel would try to move his neck, shoulders, and limbs himself. He struggled to build up his strength, while his muscles became more shrunken every day. I would watch the effort in agony, unsure of whether I wanted him to keep trying, and failing, or stop trying, and keep the hope of success. Then I, and Susan and Debbie if they were with me, would move his arms and hands and his legs for him. We would lotion them, and clean his nails. We would arrange his bed.

Daniel's arms and hands were supported by pillows. One day, to brighten up the room and his bed, Susan and I went to get special tie-dye T-shirts in his favorite colors. We put them over the pillows so that he had special, decorated pillow cases to rest his arms and hands on. In the store where we got the pillowcases, we also got some crystals. We decided the doctors weren't helping, so we would try crystals. We placed rocks at his elbows, shoulders, on his stomach. We rubbed smooth crystals over his face. I had an amethyst necklace with a silver mermaid on a crystal pendant made for him, and we draped it over his head. He laughed at us and said he'd try anything, to go ahead and enjoy ourselves.

Daniel was often very uncomfortable, and the medicines didn't seem to help much. At those times, all that he wanted was the physical sensations that he could no longer have, except on his face. For hours, each of us in turn would rub our fingers over his face, around his eyes, up one side of his nose, down the other, over his forehead, along the lines of his chin. Sometimes he liked only one or two fingers at a time, while at others he seemed to want the fuller sensation of all of our fingers. We all became comfortable with the intimacy of this special request, happy only in that we could give him relief, and comfort.

Without conscious thought, we slowly brought Daniel's favorite things to him. We had a CD player, and all of his music. Much of the day, Daniel would as usk to play music by the Grateful Dead and his other favorites. Sometimes he would ask for some of the music I liked, too. He also wanted his favorite posters. We hung them laboriously over his head: the Grateful Dead, a poster of his three favorite music stars, with the words "We still shine on," some other groups. He chose a Grateful Dead skull, with roses, as his favorite poster, to be over his head. I *hated* that poster, but, compromise on other things as he would, he refused to compromise on that.

"Please," I would beg. "It depresses me."

"Why?"

"Because it's a dead person's skull, that's why. And I can't stand it being over your head."

"Mom, you are crazy. It's just a symbol they use. It doesn't mean anything. I love that poster. I've had it for a long time."

"Please, Daniel. I know you don't understand, but can't you do me this favor? Just this one? Please!"

"No."

And the poster stayed. What thoughts, I wondered, must go through his head, looking up at that skull? Can he really separate death from the Grateful Dead symbols? I couldn't, and can't.

Trying to understand what it would be like to be a quadriplegic, I realized that perhaps he doubted the condition, or even the very existence of, his body. I asked if he wanted to see it. I began by holding up his hands and arms so that they were in his line of vision. Then I asked if he wanted me to get a mirror, so he could see his whole self. He agreed with interest. I will never forget the intensity of his concentration as he looked in the mirror and looked down at his body for the first time since his accident.

"Are you done yet?" I asked after a while.

"No. Move it down some. I can't see my feet." I adjusted the mirror and held it, my arm aching. Daniel studied himself with interest, looked at his arms on the pillow, at his face. He moved his mouth and nose, and tried to move his head a little.

"OK," he said finally. "That's enough."

"That's good, because my arm is falling off," I answered, and gratefully put the mirror down.

The mirror became another part of our everyday routine. It seemed to satisfy some inner need. It was a simple thing, but I think it helped Daniel's sense of bodily integrity, damaged though it was.

Daniels' friends visited daily. Groups of youg people would come up to the ICU, mostly in the evenings, sometimes during the day. In the first days, Daniel loved these visits. Forever the clown, with a good sense of humor, he would joke with them and move his head as he could. He would make funny faces. I don't know why, but this bothered me terribly. I didn't want to stop him from relaxing for a few moments with friends, but I didn't think he, or they, should make a joke out of this terrible situation. I never said anything, though, and, perhaps all too soon, the joking stopped.

When Daniel's loss of function increased, and he began to deal with the enormity of what had happened, he began to refuse to see any friends. I was conflicted. On one hand, I felt this was his choice, and his right. On the other, these were his friends. They loved him and cared about him, and they were faithful to him. Also, if he came back to U. of R. after rehabilitation, he would need them. They would be vital to his happiness and adjustment to school.

So, I played games with myself, with him, and with his friends. Sometimes I told them he was asleep, and couldn't see anyone. Sometimes I begged him to see them for a few minutes. In retrospect, I'm sorry I asked him to do this. But at that time, in all good conscience, I felt that I was safeguarding his future, helping him to stay close to those who cared about him, helping them to understand what had happened. These were, after all, the friends who had saved him, who had jumped in the water, who had held him up, who had called 911, who had ridden in the ambulance. Ultimately, Daniel kept control of things, anyway. If he couldn't face his friends, he would just close his eyes and go to sleep.

Daniel slept for hours and hours, every day. I think it was from the medications, in part, but also from his very real need to withdraw and escape the enormity of what had happened to him for stretches of time. At those times, I just sat by quietly, and watched him. Just watching, I could be content. I had a chair by the window, near his bed. I had his over-bed tray, lowered to chair height.

I learned to play solitaire. I read dog-eared copies of *Reader's Digest*, borrowed from the waiting room. I couldn't read anything longer than those articles. My ability to concentrate, still very much compromised today, had disappeared completely. I don't remember what else I did. Mostly, I think I just sat and looked at him.

Sometimes in the long hours that Daniel slept, I felt very alone. I was, after all, in a strange city, and I was truly alone, much of the time. During those times, the phone was my lifeline, my link to love and care and support. When he was not with me, I called Leonard every few hours. If the girls were not with me, I called them several times a day.

There were two phones in the ICU waiting room, both public. In addition to the lack of privacy, there was also discomfort when I tried to use them. The phone lines did not reach anywhere one could sit. Sometimes, I dragged a heavy chair over to the phones and tried to sit on the back. After a few minutes, that hurt, too.

The phones rang for me, for us, constantly. Often, both phones rang with calls for us, all evening. Friends from home, friends from college, friends from childhood, relatives from all over the country and overseas called. No one could believe how often the phones were for us. Other families in the ICU answered the phones if we were with Daniel, and took messages. Often, we would find eight or ten pinned to the bulletin board when we came out for a soda. I would divide up returning the calls if there was someone with me. If I was alone, I'm afraid not all of them got returned.

People were wonderful to us. They called often, and listened to my latest reports, and asked what they could do. I didn't hesitate—I gave everybody jobs. Some found out about rehabilitation, some cancelled my appointments, some cared for my house, some invited my husband to dinner, some sent packages. Later, they all said they loved this. It made them feel that, though far away, they could still do something to help. As indeed they could, and did!

I will never forget two special experiences: friends who, on two occasions, simply showed up in the ICU for a visit. These faces from home meant more than I can ever say. They were a reminder of something I seemed to have lost touch with: the rest of my world and my life. Their visits were bittersweet reminders.

Especially helpful was a new friend—a mother of classmates of my children, a teacher of Daniel's, whose oldest son had also had a diving accident and was also a quadriplegic. Years ahead of me now, she remembered all the painful, slow steps. She gave me support and encouragement, and the hope that things could really be good, as they had been for her son. It was not until several weeks later that I realized, by myself, that her son's injury was well below Daniel's current status. Her son could drive, could propel his own wheelchair, could write with an adaptive device. He could, of course breathe on his own. Discouraged, I turned away from her help. Now, I can appreciate her perseverance in offering all of the support she could.

Almost everyone in my world, it seemed, called. Almost. Some friends were notable for their silence. In retrospect, I know that their silence was not lack of love or concern, but only their own discomfort with the situation in which we now found ourselves. I understand, but the hurt remains, to this day. Some of these friends are still unable to talk with me, to relate to me. I guess that they always will be, and that, perhaps, they can no longer be friends with the person that I was then becoming, and have now fully become.

Along with the calls, mail flooded in. Cards and letters came in thick bunches every day. Some days, Daniel would let me read him all of them. Some days, he said he didn't care, and did not want to hear. Read or unread, I hung them all on the walls of his room, trying to add a note of cheer. Before much time had passed, all three walls in the room were completely covered with cards, letters, and pictures.

Those first weeks, Daniel and I lived in our own world. It was a world onto itself. It was sufficient, and not unbearable.

And, through it all, medical problems kept developing and unfolding, crises came and were resolved. He was left ever more compromised, ever more weakened.

7

My ICU Family

Though I sat with Daniel for unboken hours, times would come when I would have to leave him. I felt that it was very important to keep his sense of personal bodily privacy, and I always left the room when care had to be given. There were innumerable treatments, procedures, and x-rays, which necessitated that I leave the room. Also, when Daniel had visitors, I felt that it was important that he have some privacy. These times, I spent in the ICU waiting room.

In addition to the bareness, the dirtiness, the discomfort of the seating arrangements, and the overall unattractiveness, the two all-too-public phones, and the generally crowded circumstances, there were two other important items in the waiting room: a clock, by which I could measure sequences of time (time with Daniel, time away from Daniel), and a loudspeaker, through which families could be paged.

And they were paged continuously.

"Family of Jane Mathews," the loudspeaker would blare, and a small weary group would detach itself from the herd, and rush down the hall.

"Family of Eleanor Filbert," the next announcement would come, a scant two minutes from the preceding one.

Sometimes no one would answer.

"Family of Eleanor Filbert," the box would repeat. Everyone would look up, toward the ceiling by the door, at the box, and then look around, dully curious.

"Is there anybody from the Filbert family there?," the disembodied voice would ask, with annoyance.

"No," someone would finally reply, and silence would reign until the phone rang, or the next announcement came.

The phones were handled similarly. "Rothmans," someone would shout, and wave the receiver in our direction.

Almost everyone took turns answering the phone, the most energetic person that day bearing the lion's share of the burden. Sometimes there were torn pieces of paper for messages. Often there were not. Even when there were, pen or pencil was never supplied. The bulletin board, far from the phone, had few thumbtacks.

Sometimes the callers would be very demanding.

"What do you mean, she's not there? She's supposed to be there!" someone would insist. "Can you please look for her?"

"Can you go down to Sarah Carson's room and get her sister? I need to talk to her."

"Can you leave a message for Ward Scott?" demanded another. "Tell him that his uncle had to go to take the car to be fixed at the Exxon station on Russell Boulevard, the one next to the Burger King. I'm leaving right now, so can you please find him and tell him to pick me up from there in about twenty minutes from now? Let's see, it's eight fifteen. At about eight thirty five. Don't forget to tell him because I will be stranded there if you don't and I don't have any way to get to the hospital and see my sister if he doesn't come to get me. Oh, and could you tell him to bring my jacket? It's cold here and I left it in my sister's room. It's the brown one with the white collar. Thanks."

There was not a piece of paper on the entire floor, except in the patient's charts, large enough to write all that on! And then, of course, the receiver of the call felt obligated to find Ward Scott so that his uncle wasn't left stranded.

There were rude callers, too.

"Mary Smith, I want to talk to Mary Smith."

The receiver of the call would turn to the group and call, "Mary Smith, call for Mary Smith." No answer.

"She's not here."

"Well, go look for her."

Wearily, the telephone answerer would check the hall, the two small waiting rooms.

"She's not here."

The click of the phone as the angry caller hung up was the only response.

We all recirculated the same magazines. Everyone was under so much tension, I don't think we even realized that we were reading the same articles, over and over. I read one about a man rescued by a dog somewhere cold in the *Reader's Digest* at least three or four times before I recognized that I had read it.

Toward the end of my stay, I became a ruthless thief. I decided it was my personal job, my mission, to see to it that new magazines, filled with new stories, new ideas, new pictures, were available. I stole them from anywhere I could. If I saw a magazine lying around somewhere in passing, I picked it up. I picked magazines out of the trash baskets outside the hospital. I made occasional forays into the main waiting room next to the lobby, rolling up magazines and walking out with them under my arm. I cleaned out Leonard's supply every weekend when he arrived from Annapolis with the latest mail. I must confess, I even stole some magazines from the Ronald McDonald House, which had a wonderful supply. Over the weeks, I piled up more and more, and even threw out the old, dog-eared ones.

"This is my legacy," I would tell the others, "magazines for people to read. New ones. Fresh ones."

People *lived* in the ICU waiting room. This meant they ate there, too. There was a name of one or two restaurants posted on the board, that delivered to the waiting room. At mealtimes, everyone ordered in, or unwrapped sandwiches brought from home.

There was one table, with three Brewer chairs. We all took turns, waiting until someone finished, cleared their mess, and sat down at the dirty table. When we finished, we got up so that the next family could sit down. When I was with Leonard or the kids, we ordered Chinese food, or subs, and waited for our turn. By late in the day, the stale, uncirculated air of the waiting room reeked of everyone's breakfast, everyone's lunch, everyone's dinner.

When I was alone, I skipped all my meals and just ate junk from the machines. Often, I couldn't decide what to get. My mind didn't seem to be working right. I would stand in front of the machine and stare stupidly: did I want the Ritz Bits? the Twinkies? the Chocolate Chip cookies? the sour cream and onion potato chips? Sometimes I gave up in disgust, and just had a diet soda.

Sometimes doctors would come by and find people in the waiting room, family members with whom they needed to talk. They would perch themselves on the back of a green plastic chair, and, in full view and hearing of the entire waiting room, proceed to discuss their patient's condition. Everyone tried not to look, not to hear, not to pay attention. The times that it happened to me, I felt a terrible sense of violation. It was as though Daniel's condition, problems, progress, or lack of it, was common property. Often, it was the head of the ICU, himself, who violated his patients' and their families' privacy in this way.

Most families came and went. The turnover was quite rapid, it seemed. People came in as worried groups. Mostly, they left after triumphantly announcing, to the the rest of us beleaguered souls, that they were being "transferred to a floor." They noisily gathered up their things, and made their way to the door, pausing at the threshhold for one last, lingering, look back.

Far fewer were the families that were called to the little room off the main waiting room, to wail and cry and emerge, red-eyed, newly bereft. These sorry people were forced to walk through the full waiting room, knowing from their own experiences waiting there, that every scream, every cry, had been heard by all. A silence followed them, and a path was cleared. Was it respect, fear, or some mixture of emotions too difficult to analyze that kept us rooted, quietly staring?

With time, distinct people began to come into focus. I realized that there were some other people who did not go away, but stayed day after day. They had weary, resigned looks on their faces, and reflected the greatest terror as the bereaved processions passed them. They were the families who, like ours, were in the ICU waiting room for a long haul.

Slowly, we began to speak, to learn about each other, to develop a bond of care and responsibility. The medical establishment was cold, and distant. We were tired, worried, afraid, and, often, alone. Some of us were from far away. Though I was the only one who could not go home at all, many others drove miles each day to spend hours sitting in the waiting room, content just to be nearby, as we were content.

We slowly cemented our relationships, and, over the weeks, became "family." We worried over each other, made sure we had something to eat and something warm to drink, followed each turn for better or worse in each other's family member, comforted and wept together. We answered each others' calls, or each others' pages, with a sense of security and belonging. And when my own family called, from California or Maryland, the familiar voice of a "family" member would reassure them, if mother wasn't there, that all was well. We were adrift in a strange, unknown, and sometimes terrifying place. We clung to each other for safety.

My favorite "family" member was Andrea. Her sister had had a heart problem. She needed a complicated procedure done, and was refusing to give consent. So, she lingered in the ICU day after day, as the doctors tried to convince her to have it done. After more than a month, she finally agreed. Then, delay followed delay, as new medical problems arose. As Daniel was finally wheeled out of Strong, she was, at last, headed to surgery.

Andrea lived alone. She was strong, independent. No meals in the waiting room for her! She went to the cafeteria, she sat downstairs in the hospital lobby for a change of scene, she made friends with everyone. She arrived early in the morning, as did all "family," and settled in for the day. At night, if I was going to the Ronald McDonald House, we would walk together down the hall, take the elevator, and walk outside. We each breathed deeply of the fresh air our lungs seemed to need so desperately.

We walked across to the darkened, empty parking lot, and said goodnight. We waited for each other to get in our cars, to be sure we were safe.

One night, I had Susan with me, and Andrea left before me. I went down to the parking lot, only to find her, in tears, standing by campus security. The police car light flashed eerily across the half-empty lot, a lonely beacon.

"What happened?," I asked, thinking that she had finally gotten sick herself, with too much worry.

"Oh, Julie," Andrea started to cry, "I can't believe what I did. I tried to back out of my space and something happened. The accelerator just went off and I hit these two cars. I'm so embarrassed. I never did anything like this before in my life. I've always been a good driver."

I noticed the cars, then. Her car had obviously slammed, full force, into the rear of another, pushing it over onto its neighbor. An Audi and a Mercedes. Andrea was going to have real troubles, I could tell.

"Don't worry, Andrea," I said with an assurance I did not feel. "It's only metal. It's only money. I'll stay here with you."

"They don't know whose cars they are. They have to call the police station and take a report," she cried.

"I'll stay with you."

And stay I did, so tired myself I could hardly stand, till I could speak to the police myself in her behalf, and see her safetly on her way.

What happened to Andrea, I thought, could happen to any of us. Weariness, exhaustion, dulled senses, poor reflexes. We were all experiencing the same problems.

Another "family" was thatof a burn patient, injured in an industrial accident. The wife and son remained in the hospital all day, every day. The son was an early riser, and invariably, as I arrived and looked into the waiting room each morning, he would be seated at the table, playing solitaire. He played solitaire for hours, literally hours. His mother, the burn patient's wife, brought her knitting with her, and stayed usually until late.

Burn patients suffer terribly, and this one was in and out of consciousness, and on a ventilator, for weeks. But every day, he made a little progress, almost too little to measure, but progress nonetheless. He began to overbreathe the ventilator. They were ecstatic. I pretended joy, but was really upset inside. Why was this older man able to make ventilator progress, and Daniel was not? Why could he overbreathe, and Daniel not? Why, later, could he begin to eat food, when my beloved child could not? Then, he was out of bed for short periods. I tried hard to care about this "family," and I did, but envy always got in my way. Why, oh why, couldn't something good ever happen to us? His wife was still there, knitting, when we walked past that door for the last time.

A family came, after a week, and moved into the "death room." I couldn't believe that they could live in there. The patient was dying, of sepsis from some terrible internal infection. She had a black hand on a piece of white paper on the door of her room, a warning to all who passed by that here was danger, and death. She was young, from a Middle Eastern country, and was a doctor, herself. Her husband, also a doctor, her mother, and her two children, all lived together, day and night, in the small room. The little girls would walk around and try to play in the halls, under the watchful eye of their grandmother. They were too little to understand what was happening, but knew that they could not see their mother. Sometimes they went outside her door and cried. The husband spoke little, grateful, though, for the interest of the "family."

Her mother spoke even less, but the agony transfused her face. Her mouth, pale, was an angular slash across the haggard whiteness. Her eyes, dark and sunken deep in their sockets, reflected only flattened images. Day after day, I tried to reach her, to offer sympathy and support. I walked with her as she paced the halls, alone, unhappy, inexorably losing her dearly beloved daughter.

This family was very, very angry. They felt that not enough was being done for the patient. She was being left to die, when her life could be prolonged, they felt. They begged and pleaded with the doctors, who apparantly felt that further treatment was futile, and only prolonged the pain.

After two weeks, she finally died. No sounds of grief came from the little room. In silence, the family packed up, and moved out. Even the little girls were still at last, evidently understanding that something terrible had happened.

One little girl, about ten, stands out as a special member of the "family." Her grandmother was very ill, though I don't remember exactly what had happened to her. Her daughter, distraught, alone, came daily to the hospital and stayed for hours and hours with her mother. The little girl was left by herself in the waiting room. Never have I seen such a sweet, good little girl. She read comic books, colored, and talked to the "family." Motherless evening after evening, sitting in a green plastic chair, she touched each of us in spite of our own worries, and we reached out to her, and gave her what love and comfort we could.

Through the weeks, there were also other, less permanent "family" members. A very, very special one was a lady whose father was dying, in one of the pods in Daniel's ICU. He had lived to a "ripe old age," as she put it, in very good health. Now, he was failing and the family decided they did not want to prolong his life. Life support was to be stopped. For hours, I talked to this lady. We shared our thoughts and ideas about death, we worried over how she would survive, and we worried about Daniel, and his lack of progress. We gave each other frequent hugs, the only physical comfort afforded in those long and trying hours.

Finally, she met me in the hall to tell me that her father's time had come. She was scared, but she was going to remain by his bedside, for as long as it took. He was unconscious, but she was sure that he would be aware of her presence, and of her love. She said she had something special to tell me.

"I'm going to stand right by him," she said, "and hold his hand. I'll stay while he is dying. But I want you to know something. While he is dying, I will ask him to send his strength, and his spirit, to your Daniel. He's a strong man. He would have made it if he hadn't had complications. He will give Daniel strength. He will add his will to Daniel's."

I accepted her gift gratefully. I never saw her again, for her father died in the night, while I was asleep in Daniel's room.

One of the very best "family" members wasn't really a family member at all, but an employee. Sharon was the night house-keeper assigned to the ICU. It was her job, at the end of the day, to remove all the trash and remains of everyone's meals, and straighten out the waiting room. She was very large and very motherly and, long before we knew who she was, she had taken us, and the other "family" members, under her especial wing. She prayed over us constantly, by herself, and in church. Every night, she would greet us and listen to the reports of our day. She really cared about each of us. Once weary evening, to show my care for her, I surprised her by cleaning up the waiting room myself, and presenting her with an all-neat surprise. Sharon was amazed, and very grateful.

"But, Julie," she said, "what did you do with all the soda cans?"

"They're all in the trash," I answered proudly. "I picked up every single one for you."

She sighed.

"What's the matter?" I asked, worried that I had done something wrong.

"Nothing. Thank you. I really mean it. But I take all the cans and turn them in and get paid for recycling them. Now they're all in the trash."

So much for being helpful! But the thought was there, and, I know, appreciated.

I don't know what I would have done without my ICU family. They gave me love and strength, and even a laugh or two, in terrible, tough times.

The special thing about this "family" was that we never, never once, saw each other's ill family member. We gave love and care and concern, for people we didn't even know.

8

Losing Hope

Day followed weary day, assuming a sad routine, and still Daniel's condition did not get better. All the "have faiths" in the world didn't do any good. We waited, and we waited, and we waited, but things did not get better.

One day, in the middle of the second week, Daniel's lung tore. I didn't understand very much about it at the time. Dr. K. wanted to put in a chest tube. He said the lung would expand immediately, and would heal quickly. The tube would be out in two or three days, at most. We gave permission, and he made an enormous hole, at least four inches in length, and inserted the chest tube. The hole horrified me. It was raw and angry-looking. The tube from inside the hole was connected to some kind of box that drained bloody fluid from his lung. More x-rays, more apparatus hanging from him.

Daniel seemed weaker, too, and after the first few days, I noticed that his arms and legs seemed to be shrinking. His muscle mass was disappearing. I asked the girls if it was my imagination, but it wasn't. He got thinner and thinner, until, after too short a time, it seemed to me that only his face was the face of my beloved son.

He had high fevers, all the time. He received medicines for this, but nothing worked. The nurses and I would try to cool him down by washing his body in cold water. With much effort, his fever would drop a degree, then, after a few hours, rise again. Daniel was miserable. Apparently, one loses the ability to sweat below the level of a spinal cord injury. Perspiration is the body's air conditioning system, and Daniel's only worked at the level of his face. He would perspire heavily, drops forming as fast as my hands could wipe them off with a washcloth, clouding his vision, itching him, making his unbearably uncomfortable.

He had had a tracheotomy when it became apparant that he would not easily get off the ventilator. The hole was very large. We waited and waited for it to heal around the tube, but it didn't seem to do it. Daniel's bone graft site, from which bone had been taken during his surgery, was also not healing, and he had two open areas that required treatments. His precipitous drops in blood pressure and pulse continued to terrify us all at all hours, and he had several cardiac arrests.

Daniel also had terrible, terrible headaches, which didn't seem to be helped much by medications. I, fearful of addiction, tried hard to discourage use of strong painkillers, and several times we argued over this issue. And, of course, all of us were focussed on the ventilator problem above and beyond all else.

Far from getting off the ventilator immediately, as his surgeon had promised, Daniel seemed less and less able to assist himself with breathing. An early attempt to wean him failed completely. Every day the respiratory technicians tried to work with him, to encourage him to take breaths. We all worked with him, coached him, breathed along with him. We teased and cajoled and begged, until we realized that this was not something that Daniel could control. Of course, he wanted to get off the ventilator. Of course, he was trying.

The method Strong used to wean him was too complex for me to fully understand, but I do know that they gave him less and less oxygen, hoping that his body's need for it would force him to take an independent breath. Instead, Daniel would beg for oxygen. It seemed that he was always oxygen starved, even though they were not trying to wean him.

"Bag me," he would beg the nurses repeatedly. "I need air. I don't have enough air." And, often, they did "bag" him, giving him some pure oxygen, manually, and he would relax and seem to feel better, at least for a short while.

It is one of my great frustrations still today that, with all of our knowledge and expertise, we did not demand that a pulmonary physician oversee these attempts at ventilator weaning, which were completely managed by technicians. They were knowledgable, kind, and sympathetic, but they were not physicians. Who knows what unnecessary suffering Daniel was forced to undergo because of this.

In order to combat the fragmentation of care and try to get some semblance of order and planning for Daniel, I finally demanded a case conference. I told Daniel about it, and he requested to be present, so that it was conducted at his bedside. I understand that I was well within my rights to request such a conference, within care guidelines of the hospital. I requested all of the doctors caring for him (and there were many, many, they tell me), Dr. K., his nurse, the respiratory technician, the speech therapist who was working on his swallowing, and the physical therapist.

Those who came were: Dr. K., the physician therapy technician, the speech pathologist, the respiratory technician, his nurse, and two psychologists. Not one of his physicians attended, responded, or communicated with me in any way. *Not one.*

Daniel and Susan had prepared Daniel's questions. They included requests for a review of his medications, for drink and food, for pain medication. He also wanted to know when he could expect his function to come back, when he would get off the ventilator, and when he could go to the toilet by himself.

With pain tearing at my heart, I slowly read the questions. Dr. K. answered them as best he could. He reviewed the medications, arranged for him to try taking some nourishment by mouth with the speech pathologist, adjusted his pain medications. He told him he did not know when his function would come back, but that it surely would. It always did return to the

level on admission. He just had to be patient. Attempts to get
Daniel off the ventilator would continue. The toilet question,
most pathetic of all, he deferred by saying it would be addressed
once Daniel was in rehabilitation.

The conference could change little, despite the good will of
those who attended. Daniel's function did not return. He
could not even move his head from side to side, not even a little bit. It was supported with rolls of towels by each ear, which
made him hotter than ever when he was feverish. He greedily
began to drink—Snapple was his favorite, and Susan made
sure he had plenty of it—and, slowly, to eat. He ate jello and
pudding and mashed potatoes. He sucked on lollypops. Soon,
however, we began to notice that the food was seeping heavily
out of the tracheotomy, and onto his chest. It was not going
down to his stomach. All food and drink was stopped immediately, and Daniel was back where he had been—ice chips on
occasion only. Though attempts to wean him from the ventilator continued, no progress was made. Rather, Daniel continued to seem less and less able to make any attempt to breathe.

"Face it, Mom," he said to me one day, "I'm ventilator
dependent. I'm never going to get off this."

"Don't say that, Daniel," I begged, tears coming quickly to
my eyes, "You just have to try very hard. You'll get off. Everyone says you will. And your shoulders will come back, and
you'll be better."

"No, mom," he answered sadly, "I won't. I know I won't."

It was around this time that I had a strange experience with
one of the nurses. As I've said, I loved all the nurses that took
care of Daniel. Only with two of them, in all of our time at
Strong, were there ever any problems. This was one of them.

Susan came out to the waiting room one day, and told me
Daniel was very agitated. No one could calm him down. He
was biting his tongue. He was biting so very hard that blood was
running down his chin, and this had upset the nurse. Daniel
wasn't "saying" anything, just biting hard. I went in to see him.
He was calmer, feeling the pain medication that the nurse had

given to him. Eventually, I was able to persuade him to stop biting his tongue.

That evening, in the hall, before I left, I jokingly said to the night nurse caring for him,

"Take good care of him. Don't let him bite his tongue."

"He can bite it if he wants to," she answered.

"*What?*," I was amazed.

"It's his body," she insisted. "He can decide what he wants to do with it. If he wants to bite his tongue off, he has that right."

"I can't believe this," I said in amazement. "You mean if he tries to bite his tongue off, and you see him do it, you would just *let* him."

"That's right."

"Well, don't. I think he has enough problems without having a bitten-off tongue."

"Everyone has the right to do what they want to themselves," she maintained stubbornly.

"He's sick. He's taking medication. Do you have children?"

"I have a boy, six."

"Would you let him bite off his tongue, if he wanted to?"

"Of course I would. He can do whatever he wants to himself."

"I can't believe it. Isn't that what you are for, his mother? To keep him from hurting himself?"

"No."

"Well," I said, giving up, "Daniel isn't your child. He's mine. And I do not think it is in his best interests to bite his tongue off. So please put a washcloth in his mouth if he tries."

"We'll see," she said grudgingly. And I could not get any further with her.

Daniel did not try to bite his tongue again.

But his frustration continued to build, as I desperatly sought for a rehabilitation facility for him, and argued with my insurance company. He was aware of my search, and my problems. He wanted to believe that he could improve, that somewhere there was a place that could help him. But things kept getting worse.

A few days after the tongue episode, Daniel began to say that he wanted to die. He told his sister, and he told the nurse, who told Dr. K.

In the unprivacy of the ICU waiting room, Dr. K. approached me with Daniel's request. We sat on the green plastic chairs by the telephones.

"He wants to die. I can understand that. Living like that is the worst thing that can ever happen to somebody. I can understand that he wants to die. I would want to die too. I think we should consider his request. His condition is the absolute worst thing I can think of, and I see many terrible things in this ICU."

I was outraged.

"How can you say that?" I countered, furious that he was really serious. "You have no right. Just because *you* would want to die if you were a quadriplegic doesn't mean Daniel should. Lots of quads lead very fulfilling lives. He says this now, but he hasn't had any rehab. He hasn't tried. He doesn't even know what his function level will be, finally. He doesn't know how he'll feel off the ventilator, and everyone says he'll get off it."

"I just can't imagine how he could want to live."

"*You* don't have to imagine. *He* does. And he doesn't have the knowledge out of which to make a decision. He doesn't know what's out there. You could never tell me that, at this point, Daniel could give informed consent. He's not informed. And he's here, in this ICU. He's on medications. He has no idea what his potential is, now."

"That's true, he doesn't."

"If Daniel wants to die," I said, fully meaning every word, "I will not stop him. I will support him and give him all the love and care I can. I will understand. But not now. Not yet. Let him go on to a rehabilitation facility first. I'm trying to get him to Craig Hospital, in Denver. It's supposed to be the best. If, after he goes there, and learns all that he can do, he still wants to die, I will know it will be the right choice."

I went back to Daniel's room.

"Dan," I said seriously, "I hear you want to die."

"I can't live like this, Mom. I'm too dependent. I hate being dependent. And my head hurts all this time. It hurts when I get suctioned. I don't have enough air to breathe and I feel like I'm going to die anyway, from having no air. It's horrible like this."

"I know, Dan. I understand. But I ask you to just give me some time. I'm trying to arrange for you to leave here and go to Craig Hospital. You know that. I'm going as fast as I can. I think we'll be able to work it out. They will have to come here and see you, because you are on the ventilator. But I'm working on arrangments. Will you wait, Dan? Will you wait until we get to Craig?"

"All right, Mom. I'll try. I don't want to die. But I don't want to live like this. I'll wait and try Craig."

And so, it was decided.

9

Finding Hope, and Losing it Again

Part of my "deal" with Daniel involved moving him from Strong to a rehabilitation facility as soon as possible. We had chosen Craig Hospital, in Denver. With direct pressure from Leonard, our primary insurance company decided to accept this. However, they refused to pay the cost of transportation, and precious days were lost arguing and arranging. It would cost $10,000 to fly Daniel to Denver. Frustrated and angry, we finally decided to go ahead with plans and somehow assume the cost ourselves, if it was necessary. After we did that, our two warring insurance companies finally agreed: they would split the cost.

Because Daniel was on a ventilator, Craig would not accept him without a personal evaluation by one of their physicians and their admissions coordinator. We arranged the trip to Rochester, and the visit to Daniel at Strong.

As the day approached, I got more and more excited. Help was on the way, I thought, and spinal cord injury expertise. I counted the hours and the minutes, and my spirits flew high— higher than they had been since Daniel's accident. Things would be all right, I was sure. The saviors were coming.

Daniel tried hard, but he did not share my optimism. He continued to complain of pain. He continued to withdraw quietly. He continued to have episodes of low pulse and blood pressure. He all but gave up weaning from the ventilator, feeling that he was not capable. And, through it all, he begged constantly for more air. Finally Dr. K., unable to watch Daniel in so much pain, prescribed much stronger medications.

Before my very eyes, the day before the visitors from Denver were to arrive Daniel seemed to fade away. His eyes glazed over. He could hardly open them. His "speech," the mouthing of words with which he communicated, became slow and slurred. He had continual involuntary movements with his mouth, suggestive to me of tardive dyskenesia. I knew it couldn't happen so quickly. But, I also knew it happened from the medications he was on, and that it was very serious. He didn't even ask for more air.

I was alone in Rochester, and desperate. What would the doctor say, when he saw Daniel? What if he got rejected? I laughed and told myself this was, really, much more serious than getting rejected from college, or from the medical schools that were fading daily farther into the distance. I wanted him to make a good impression. Instead, he was at his worst.

I was at Strong waiting the next morning when Dr. M. and the admissions coordinator arrived. It seemed to me that a halo of light surrounded them. They brought it with them as they entered my embattled world, lifting the seige. They were tanned, and healthy. They inspired confidence. And they came from the place where miracles happened. They entered the dirty, dark brown and green plastic world of Strong, seemingly comfortable and at ease with it.

The admissions person spoke with Daniel and I, while Dr. M. reviewed his chart. Daniel wanted to listen, to pay attention, to respond. I could see that he was trying as hard as he could. But the medicines were stopping him, dulling his senses, slowing his responses. When Dr. M. came to examine him, I waited outside, fearful, anxious, hopeful.

When they were all finished, we had a conference in the small, airless room off the hallway: Dr. M., the admissions coordinator, Dr. K., and I. The two psychologists also came in, crowding the room to standing-room-only. Dr. M. began the conference by saying that he had evaluated Daniel, and had found him to be a C-1, not a C4-5. Neurologically, he said, he was a C-1. I remember staring at him in disbelief. No, I cried. No. He can't be. They said he was a C4-5. It's not true. It's the medication—he's on so much medication.

Never have I felt so alone. Five people stared at me, measuring me, watching my reactions. They looked at me closely, competently, professionally— pityingly.

I looked at the two psychologists, safe from responsibility of any kind. They were just there, it seemed to me, to watch me. I couldn't stand it. I had to keep the people from Craig. I had to keep Dr. K. But I didn't have to have them staring at me. All of their kindness to me over the time I had been at Strong disappeared from my mind and heart for that moment.

"Please leave," I said to them, trying to be calm. "There are too many people in here. I think it would be helpful to me if you would leave."

They left. It helped.

Carefully, Dr. M. explained his findings. I didn't hear. My mind was still saying, "C-1, C-1." I was terrified.

He explained about the ventilator weaning techniques. The doctors at Craig had done research and developed a method of weaning where they gave the patients a great deal of air. I didn't hear the rest of the procedure. My mind stopped there.

"Please," I said, interrupting the doctors' conversation about the techniques. "Daniel is suffering so much from the lack of air. If it's all going to be changed any way, could we stop the suffering now? Right now? Could you please go and tell them," I said to Dr. K., "so he won't suffer another second."

And Dr. K. went, and changed the order.

Dr. M. told me that they would accept Daniel and try to work with him. I was desperately grateful for the opportunity that he offered, and for the willingness to take on what he described as an atypical spinal cord injury patient, whose symptoms and course were unusual and difficult to interpret. Daniel was, actually, still too unstable to enter rehabilitation. He would go first to the Neurotrauma Unit of Swedish Hospital, next door to Craig. He would have Craig medical personnel, but also the diagnostic and recuperative resources he still needed. He would go in another week's time.

Because of Daniel's unstable pulse and blood pressure, Dr. K. wanted to put in a pacemaker. Dr. M. disagreed. He felt that this would prevent any future MRI's and therefore limit diagnostic capabilities in Denver. He felt that Daniel could be managed with ventilator adjustments, as the drops were always associated with a decrease in blood oxygen levels. No decision was reached.

Too soon, it was time for them to leave. I watched them walk away from me, down the hall, surrounded by their halo of light and hope. And I was left again, alone with my problem.

Left, for one more week.

That evening, by phone, Leonard and I made a momentous medical decision. We requested that Daniel be taken off all medications except those clearly serving a biological, life-sustaining function. I told him that his Dad and I had talked and had agreed that we could not let him continue in this stuporous state. It was frightening, but I did it, approaching first the nurse, and then the doctor, with my request.

I watched him for hours through that night, fearful of the responsibility I had taken upon myself. By morning, Daniel was alert and responsive again, even smiling at me as I kept talking excitedly about the trip to Denver, and the possibilities that I envisioned for him there. By afternoon, the involuntary mouth movements had stopped. That evening, we watched television again.

Daniel's pulse and blood pressure continued to be a problem. When he was turned on his side, they would drop. When he was suctioned, they would drop. If the ventilator hose came undone, which happened periodically, they dropped instantly and precipitously. He could not tolerate the slightest drop in his oxygen level. Levels that would be tolerated easily by a healthy person were lethal to him. Finally, exhausted from the frequency of these terrifying moments of near-death, I agreed to a temporary pacemaker, inserted through a vein in his chest.

Dr. K. said it was absolutely necessary for Daniel to have a permanant pacemaker inserted before transfer. He could easily, he felt, die on the airplane, where the facilities for reviving him, should there be an incident, were minimal. Did I want to be responsible, he asked, for his death on the plane enroute to Denver? He would not discharge him without it. Far from Dr. M.'s guidance, I gave in, cutting off forever any ability to examine the area of injury with MRI, the clearest diagnostic method.

Dr. K.'s rotation at Strong ended, for me, very abruptly, shortly thereafter. He had not wanted to upset me by informing me earlier, but he said goodbye to Daniel and me, assuring us that someone would assume responsiblity for him. If someone did, I was never aware of that. We were abandoned. In my mind I felt we were purposely and consciously abandoned because we had chosen to leave, because I had asked for the ventilator setting change, and the medication changes. I know that's probably not true, but that was how I felt.

We were on our own. We had five days to go.

10

I Will Get My Son out of This Hospital Alive

During those last days at Strong, my "seige" mentality developed, blossomed, and flowered, unchecked, as we were ignored by the medical community. Rotations were changing, people were going on vacation, and familiar faces everwhere seemed to be replaced with strangers. I felt as though Daniel was being left to die and that, if I did not watch carefully, he would.

My only allies, during those dark, dark days, were the nurses. They seemed to truly want him to make it to Denver. I could almost imagine them saying to themselves "Not on my shift—he won't die on my shift." They were kind, and good to us.

Leonard arrived, for his last visit in Rochester. While Daniel kept insisting that he wanted all of his things to remain in his house in Rochester, because he was coming back to it, I felt that this was not a good plan. If he made it back, I thought, we would be thrilled to bring all of his things back. If he didn't, I wanted to protect myself, and Leonard, from having to come back up to get them.

I approached Daniel with this, one of the very few decisions that I ever imposed on him during the course of his illness. I went over all the plans, and all his choices. I went over our projected time frame. I assured him that we would bring all of his things back when he returned, if indeed he decided that he wanted to return. But I said that his father was taking them, and his car, home.

There was much less argument than I expected. He only asked that we leave a few things, such as his stereo cabinet, for his housemates to enjoy. We were happy to oblige.

On that last Saturday in Rochester, I sorted all his clothes with a friend of his, setting aside and packing up the things that were to go with us to Denver. T-shirts, shorts, shirts that buttoned for ease of access, underwear, socks, jacket. From that other lifetime, eerie memories assailed me. It felt like getting him ready for camp.

I never went to the house where the accident happened, but Leonard had to do that. He packed up the car with all Daniel's college belongings, all of his treasures.

The goodbyes were terrible. Leonard was not going to see us for several weeks. I was feeling abandoned. As we walked together for the last time down the hall, after he had said goodby to Daniel, the phone rang for us, again. It was Susan.

"I know this is a terrible morning for you," she began.

I was crying.

"I'm going to be all alone," I cried into the phone, in the unprivacy of the hall, "and I'm worried about Dad driving all that way alone with all of Daniel's things. It will be terrible for him. And you know how he drives. He'll fall asleep without me, and have an accident, and get killed. I wish I could go with him. But I can't leave Daniel."

Susan listened, and cried too.

"Mom," she said, "I knew you would be very upset today so Michael and I decided to tell you something, even if it's very very early. We're having a baby. It's just three weeks, but we thought it would cheer you up."

"Susan, how wonderful. When are you due?"

"In April. You can tell Daniel. He's going to be an uncle in April."

"I will," I promised. And, it did help, a little. I would have been so happy, so excited, in other times, other places. Here, the joy was met with the harsh reality of hallway and waiting room, elevator, and goodbye. And Leonard was gone.

Daniel seemed happy with the news. But for him, as for me, it was news that belonged to another time and another place. He would never hold the baby, himself. He would never play ball with it, take it anywhere, hold its hand. He would, if he stayed on the ventilator, never be able to talk to it. "Uncle Daniel" would not be the kind of uncle he wanted to be.

As night came, that Sunday, we made a pact. We had three more days, until Wednesday. We would stay together. We would keep our spirits up. We would make it through. We would get out of Strong, together, alive. We would meet whatever was ahead.

Over the next few days, we admitted to each other that we were both scared. We did not like Strong, but it was safe. The room was familiar, the nurses were supportive. We knew the equipment and how it worked, and the routine of the hospital. We also had all the support of Daniel's fraternity brothers, and Susan's in-laws. We would be going into a new world, where we knew no one, in a city where we had never been. We could not even begin to imagine what was ahead of us. Would people be nice? Would the room be comfortable? Would they let me stay as much as I wanted? Where was I going to be? What would Daniel be doing in rehabilitation?

And, worst of all, for me—what if he stayed a C-1? What if even Craig, the miracle place, could not help him to have a life that was tolerable for him? What then? There *was* nowhere else, no further things to try or places to go. I had fought and fought for this and had gotten what I wanted so desperately. Now I worried that it still would not be enough.

The next night, Daniel had a cardiac arrest, even with the temporary pacemaker. He was scheduled to have the permanant one placed the next morning. The chief of the ICU met me in the hall to tell me that the temporary pacemaker had shifted, inside of Daniel, so that it was not working. When the nurse turned him on his side for care, he arrested. He seemed to me to be as cold and uncaring as ever a person can be to a lonely, terrified, mother. He seemed annoyed at Daniel, as though he was purposely creating problems which he, the chief, had to solve. But he reinserted it correctly, and said we should count the hours until morning.

In the darkened room, I sat in my corner. I strained my eyes toward the monitor, and watched the lines: red lines, green lines, yellow lines. By the strength of my staring at them, I thought magically, I would keep them steady. If I took my eyes off them, terrible things would happen. All through the night, I stayed awake and stared. Nothing happened, and at 7:00 A.M. they came and took him away. I had made it. He had survived. I slept.

On the last day, we took the room apart. We took down all the cards, and all the presents, and all the posters. Some things we would take to Denver. Some things the social worker would mail to Annapolis. Daniel's friends came to help us pack, to say goodby, to visit for the last time. There were promises of trips to Denver, of keeping his things for him, of writing and calling. It was a time of sadness, a time of hope.

The room was bare again—an ICU room, no longer Daniel's. I could already imagine the next person coming into it. Would it be somebody old and sick? Would they make the room theirs, as we had? Would their family love them and stay with them and care? Or would they be alone? Would they stay a day? An hour? A month? How quickly would all the nurses stop thinking of it as "Daniel's room"? I stared at the walls, through the door to the nurses' station, out of the window. I wanted to impress each detail in my brain. I wanted to be able to remember.

11

Westward Bound

With a turbulent mixture of apprehension and hope, I entered Strong for the last time. Goodbye, I whispered to the lobby, the gift shop. Goodbye, I called down the hall to the cafeteria. The elevator was crowded, as usual. We stood in silence, facing the door, well-trained in elevator manners. No one knew that this was my last ride up.

The nurse and respiratory technician were already there, preparing the stretcher and the ventilator that would take Daniel to Denver. One of our favorite nurses was hovering over him, getting ready, saying goodbye. His friends arrived for a last farewell, and we closed the boxes of what was to go, and what was to stay. He was transferred to the stretcher, looking like a little face in a cocoon, "safe and warm," as the children used to say.

A small audience lined the hall near his room, cheering us on and wishing us well. We passed the waiting room. Incurious faces turned toward us, immersed in the day's routine of magazines and coffee cups. Our "family" came to say goodbye, and to give us their love. Sharon from housekeeping hugged us, crying. Daniel's friends joined the procession. And the elevator came and we went down and out of the building into the fresh air and on to the ambulance.

At last, this moment that I had so desperately prayed for, begged for, worked for, was here. Everything was in place, the final goodbyes said. As we pulled out of the parking lot, Daniel's friends crowded the exit, waving and calling to us. I stopped looking, for my eyes clouded with tears. I had been so unhappy here, I thought, and yet, perversely, I was afraid to leave. Goodbye, I said to myself. Somehow, I knew that I would never, ever, be back again.

The sleek, white Learjet waited for us in a special corner of the airport. Daniel was loaded on, secured in place. His IVs were hung from the bulwark. His respirator was placed next to him. I took my place at the back, by his feet, while the nurse and respiratory technician sat at his side. I wanted to be with him, too. But, in the scale of things, I was the least essential person.

From my seat, I could barely make out his face. He was still, and silent, aware but not participating in what was happening. If I was scared, I thought, as we took off down the runway, how much more scared must he be? He was totally in the hands of two strangers, going to an unknown place. My heart went out to him and I held and squeezed his foot, trying to reassure him all the while knowing that he was not feeling my touch.

I sat back on the soft seat. I read magazines thoughtfully provided, and had a nice lunch. I slept a while, exhausted. I did everything I normally do on planes and it seemed bizarre, out of place, on this plane.

In that quiet hiatus between two worlds, I wondered about what had happened, and what was about to happen, to us. How could it be that my son, strong and healthy and full of life, was lying here, packaged neatly, unable to move, forever? This was my son, the little boy I loved, always exploring, always dirty, with patches on his knees, asking for Spaghettios and Hershey syrup, and digging to China for dinosaur bones. This was my son, going off to school neatly with his shirt and coat and tie, and coming home, shirt hanging, coat in a ball wrapped with the tie, asking for chocolate chip cookie dough and milk. My son, whose football and lacrosse games I watched for hours, cheering until I was hoarse, hiding my eyes when he fell, unable to watch him hurt. My son, who sometimes drank beer surreptitiously with his friends and hid the empty cans under the deck

where, he felt, I would never see them. My son, who still loved
to get care packages, went to Florida on spring breaks, and
studied on the topmost floor of the stacks in the library, where
he could "see the world." My son, who called me up from college in the middle of the night to discuss whether the Universe
was random and chaotic or determined and organized. How
could this be, my son? I asked his feet silently.

And what was to be? What would be in store for us? I never
had time to think about myself, and what my life was going to
be. Would I still be able to teach? To consult? To write? Would
I want to? I would enjoy being with Daniel so much, and could
even look forward to it, in a way. But how could I, I asked
myself. That was a selfish thought—I should want him to be on
his own. He needed a life of his own, not a life connected to
mine by need and dependence.

Too soon, we arrived in Denver. Feeling too exhausted to
cope with all the new things that awaited us, I sat silently next to
the driver of the ambulance on the trip to Swedish, as we passed
block after block of neat houses, manicured lawns, houses with
people whose lives were much like mine had been, before.

It all felt unreal. What was I doing here in Denver—me, Juliet
Rothman, who had never been here before—riding in the front
seat of an ambulance to an unknown destination, with my son
lying behind me, unmoving, ventilator hissing softly?

12

Entering Paradise

My first impression of paradise was of cleanness, brightness, modernness, and cheeriness. The neurotrauma unit, where Daniel was admitted, was furnished in modern pastels. It had a physical therapy area, an activities area, and social services right down the hall. It had an accessible central nursing station, even a laundry, and kitchen. From the darkness of Strong, the light was overpowering and, in the beginning, it dimmed my sight much like coming out into the bright sunshine from a dark room causes temporary blindness.

Everybody had his or her own room. Daniel's was right by the nurses' station. It had his familiar bed, a small moveable TV suspended from the wall, a nightstand, dresser, comfortable visitor's chair, closets, and a bathroom. It even had, *mirabile dictu*, a telephone. It was a room one could make one's own, if one worked around all the equipment that Daniel still, of course, needed.

New faces popped in and out with friendly smiles as we began to set up. We hung the posters, and I unpacked real clothing into real drawers and closets. I put music and books and familiar objects around, making it cosy and comfortable. Daniel seemed in good spirits, directing all of our activities carefully. I called Leonard, the girls, and friends. I could give a phone number that was ours, and sit in a chair while I spoke. Soon, we even got a headphone so that Daniel could "talk" on the telephone.

I was so happy I felt as though I was floating on air. Everyone seemed so experienced with Daniel's kind of problem. And then, to add to the miracle, a doctor came and introduced himself as Dr. B., Daniel's doctor! He had actually read Daniel's chart, and knew his problems and condition! This was the most reassuring of all. And then Dr. P. came and introduced himself as Daniel's pulmonologist. A pulmonologist to manage his breathing! I couldn't believe it! Both doctors listened to my concerns, examined Daniel, and assured me that they would be involved daily with his care!

In the midst of this excitement and relief, I felt the need to voice the committment I had made to Daniel at Strong. Daniel would work very hard, I told Dr. B. We would wait and see and hope that some function would return, and that he would be able to breathe independently. We had every confidence that everything that could be done, would be done. However, if things stayed as they were, I said, there was a good chance that Daniel would want to die. I explained his feelings while he was at Strong. I said that Leonard and I would support his decision, if he decided to have his ventilator support removed.

While I felt the need to share this, it was only one small note of caution, one very small dark cloud on the horizon in the midst of the sunshine. My heart was singing. Daniel finally had doctors I could see and talk with. Doctors who were specialized in his problems, knowledgeable, wise, and concerned. How could he do anything but improve?

Even the two problems that developed almost immediately did not upset me, for I was sure that they would quickly be resolved. Neurotrauma had several devices to serve as call bell triggers for quadriplegics. The tech tried one, another, and another, encouraging and explaining. But Daniel could not operate them. He was now in a private room, not a pod. He had no monitors. And he could not call for help. We lay the devices aside, and a tech was assigned to remain with him during the night. I was assured that this was routinely provided to neurotrauma patients in this new environment until they became accustomed to it. I was sure that Daniel would be able to operate a calling device eventually, and be "on his own." However, he could not, then, and he was very frightened. The constant presence of the techs was necessary and very, very, reassuring.

His second immediate problem was the presence of blood clots, discovered within a few hours of admission. I had not known that these could be a problem—it was one of the few complications that had not arisen at Strong. Daniel was placed on medication, and was told that he would have to remain prone, in bed, for seven to ten days. This, of course, would delay beginning rehabilitation. While I was anxious to begin, I could accept this delay in good spirits, as could Daniel.

We could *not* accept in good spirits another situation. The hospital apparently had lay ministers who routinely visited new patients and, within an hour or two of Daniel's admission, one such lay minister came to see him. This lady stood over his bed and began a conversation with the tech about *her* son, going into his senior year of college, applying at that moment to medical school. He was so smart, she gushed, so handsome. And he was going to go right to medical school. She did not look at, or interact, with Daniel or with me. The tech became involved in this conversation. He, too, it appeared, was planning to go to medical school, though not as imminently. The two talked on. I tried to introject that Daniel, too, was interested in medicine, and had in fact been in the process of applying to school. They did not notice, or respond, but just talked on. I didn't know what to do: I didn't want to listen, I didn't want Daniel to hear, but I was in a new place, and did not want to begin on a difficult note by complaining of their insensitivity. After what seemed to me to be an interminable period of time, but was probably just ten minutes, I noticed that Daniel had tears rolling down his cheeks. Furious, I found the courage to speak.

"I really do not think that we want to hear this conversation. We don't want to listen. Perhaps you could continue it outside."

The minister looked at me blankly.

"Certainly," she said, and withdrew with no apology, no further word.

"I'm so sorry," the embarrassed tech apologized, red-faced and shaken, aware of the hurt and the damage he had unwittingly caused.

While I forgave him, I could never really forget, and the pain of that experience is as raw today as I write this as it was then.

Comforting Daniel, I left him with the excuse of getting something to drink. Tears were flowing as I approached the nurses' station, still as bright and cheery and busy as it had been a few short hours before, on admission.

"I need to talk to my husband privately," I told the nurse, "I've just had a very bad experience."

"Come in here," she led me to the nurse's lounge area, "You can talk here."

"Thanks," I sobbed.

"Can you tell me what happened?"

I told the story as best I could, and added,

"I think somebody should tell the chaplain's office. I don't think that was right."

"I'll make sure to tell them."

But I never heard about it again and, after another encounter which was difficult with another lay minister the next day, I finally requested that we have no ministerial visits, citing religious differences, rather than the truth.

The hospitals maintain wonderful housing facilities for families. Right across the street from the hospital, full apartments are provided for the use of out-of-town family members. Such a one had been arranged for me and, at midnight, I went to my new "home," leaving my son in his.

All the amenities were provided. There were lists of local businesses, a yellow pages, even a supermarket that delivered, and a list of the products that they carried. There was a phone, too, and I could use it to check on Daniel as well as to call family and friends. The privacy of it all was wonderful, and, after a month of public living, it helped a great deal.

I was still alone, however. Alone in this new world, and, as I lay that first night in an unfamiliar bed, I wondered what the next few days would bring. Exhausted, I soon fell asleep and did not even wake in the night to call and check on Daniel, as I had done from the Ronald McDonald house when he was at Strong.

The next days brought—another trip to the ICU. Dr. P. found problems in Daniel's lungs which required surgical intervention. I sat again, in another waiting room, while my son underwent surgery. Bright and cheerful it was, but still fear and loneliness oppressed me. Susan was with me, having flown in to spend a few days with us, but she lay on the couch (a comfortable one, this time) and slept, tired from her second month of pregnancy. I sat and stared at the clock, tense, frightened, and feeling alone and responsible for whatever could happen.

He was to have stayed in the ICU for a day, two days at most. He stayed six. Somehow, Daniel always had the hardest of all possible times, the worst of all possible conditions, every possible complication. He had constant fevers which a doctor treated. He continued to have blood problems, and another doctor for these. He slept, with the ventilator whooshing quietly in the semi-darkness.

The ICU at Swedish was incredibly different than the one at Strong. Everything was new, modern, simple and yet functional. Each patient had a large room with glass wall arranged semicicularly around a large nurses' station. All the charting was computerized, and there was a terminal in each room. Everything was as different as different could be except for one thing: the nurses were as wonderful at Swedish as they had been as Strong.

And then the six days were over, and we moved triumphantly back to Neurotrauma, to Daniel's new "home."

At the end of our second week at Swedish, Leonard arrived, and we had a detailed conference on Daniel's condition, with Daniel present. We reviewed x-rays, medical reports, what had been done so far, and what could be planned for the future. We discussed his personal care needs, his schedule, his physical limitations. His condition was described as it was at that time: no definitive statements were made about the future. It was felt that Daniel needed some time, and better health, before any assessments could be made definitively. He was encouraged to report any changes in his condition. All of his caregivers were there: doctors, therapists, nurses, and others. We could ask questions, and voice concerns, to people who knew Daniel, and who cared about him. I asked about speech, and eating and drinking, and therapy, and transfer to Craig. I was afraid to ask about breathing.

Daniel did not have any questions.

"Did you think the conference was helpful, Daniel?" I asked after it was over, and he was settled once more in his bed.

"I guess so."

"What did you think?"

"I think I learned things I didn't know before."

"What did you learn?"

He refused to answer.

And, every day, I walked from my apartment, up to Craig. I watched the patients leaning back in their wheelchairs on the lawns, taking in the sun. I watched them talking and joking around the front steps. Everyone was in a wheelchair. Is it so much to ask, I said to the sun, raising my face to its warmth? Is it so much to ask, just that he be like this? In the sun, outside, talking with others?

I came into the dimness of Craig and took the elevator downstairs. I passed the cafeteria where I hoped Daniel would someday eat. I walked along the tunnel, passed a door, and passed from the dream of Craig to the reality of Swedish. I followed the marked path to the elevator, and up to his floor.

Late at night, I did it in reverse. I kissed him goodnight and walked the long tunnel corridor to Craig. I passed into the silence of the sleeping world of rehabilitation. How many more times, I would say to myself, will I do this before Daniel is here, in Craig, and I don't have to be in this tunnel, to walk this deserted hall so late in the night?

Daniel was actually able to begin rehabilitation. At first, this consisted just in efforts to be up, for such a long period of lying down as he had undergone since his injury creates difficulties when one first tries to get up. Days assumed a pattern: we visited in the morning, and then Daniel went to the physical therapy area. We stayed there a while, and returned to his room. He took regular naps. He "talked" on the phone. I read to him. We planned a visit to Craig's facilities. His friends were coming to visit. His sister Debbie was coming, and then Susan again. His uncle was coming. Most mornings he chose movies, and at night we watched them.

I got a map so we could see what was around us, where we were, and carefully showed Daniel the cities, roads, and towns of Colorado. I got a book with beautiful pictures of the mountains, of the aspen trees, and planned trips for when Daniel could be out with us for the day. It was going to be nice to explore a new place. We had so much to look forward to.

... 13

The Sunshine on Our Faces

Daniel progressed slowly, but it seemed to us that some progress was being made. From lying in bed, he moved to sitting in the chair, always with the back at a good angle, for short periods of time. This was "rehab." This was, we felt, the first steps.

Daniel was taken to sit in his chair in the physical therapy area, where his ventilator was connected. It was his first opportunity to see other patients in neurotrauma. For the first few days, he looked but said nothing.

I looked at what he saw, at his new peer group, trying to see it through his eyes. There was a gentleman who had brain damage. He could walk around freely, and wandered around the unit with a tech following a few steps behind. He could not be left unsupervised. There was a girl who sat in a wheelchair, staring blankly ahead, head tipped back at an angle. She did not respond or move in any way, and her breathing support system discharged a haze over her head. There was a lady who was learning to work with her hands, with a knit cap on her head, who always looked down at her knees and did not speak.

Without discussing his feelings with me, Daniel asked to be placed in a corner of the room, facing a large fish tank. He enjoyed watching the fish and could concentrate on them—their movements, their colors, their habits, he said. I promised him that we could get a beautiful fish tank when he finished rehab. He liked this idea. Looking at fish relaxed him, he said.

He felt very strongly about where he was placed. One day, "his" spot was occupied, and he was placed elsewhere in the room. He became quite upset, and, finally, told me he couldn't bear to see the other patients. He liked the fish tank, in part, because it shielded him from the view of the others. He didn't want to feel that he was like them in any way. I tried to help him, saying that each person's injury was unique and different, and each person was being helped by being here. He didn't care.

And then, a special day came. We went outside, in the wheel-chair, for the first time! We were quite a procession: Daniel, in the chair, with me pushing him, the tech who was caring for him, pulling his IV pole, the respiratory technician, pulling his portable ventilator, and Leonard. Daniel could only "sit" at a thirty-degree angle. In his chair, his six-foot height and leanness was strongly accentuated, seeming to stretch out forever, diffi-cult to maneuver through doors and around corners. But I didn't care. He was outside!

We went to the garden between the two hospitals. For the first time, Daniel could see Craig, from the outside, with its ter-race of umbrella tables. He could see the hospital where he was. He could see a beautiful garden with a pond, fish, and turtles. There were pleasant places to sit, and he chose his spot himself. This was his moment, and he made this very clear. It was not a moment for talking, or sharing, or even just being with others. He placed himself so that he could not see any of us, his "sup-port group." He wanted to be by himself. I was grateful that he had this moment, and respected his privacy.

In spite of this seeming progress, problems continued, devel-oped, and grew. He continued to be completely ventilator dependent. When he was tested, there was not the slightest hint of any ability to breathe. The constant need for suctioning, which was very painful to him, was upsetting. I made a sign for his wall to ask the techs to be extra gentle with him. Most of them were, but some weren't, and Daniel winced horribly. His skin became dry and hard, and peeled off his hands and feet. We got special balm which seemed to help. His eating and drinking was still very much unresolved. At first, he could not have a swallow test because he could not sit up. Then, there were scheduling problems. This was a very high priority for me, for I felt that eating and drinking was something that he wanted, and could enjoy very much, but I could not seem to get it resolved as day followed day. Blood clots remained a concern as well.

Daniel continued to have raging fevers, seemingly uncontrolled, indicating some underlying infection which was difficult to pinpoint and isolate. Every day, his infectious disease specialist came to see him. Every day, he leaned over Daniel's bed and stared at him, deep in thought. He tried medication after medication, but nothing seemed to work. Finally, he decided to order a very powerful medicine called amphoterracin. It was to be administered daily. It was light-sensitive, and had to be covered with a dark plastic bag.

For some admittedly irrational reason, I developed an immediate aversion to this medicine. It was too strong. I didn't want Daniel to have it. Every day I would beg the doctor to stop it, and every day he would reason with me that this was the best medicine to use, if we wanted to stop the fevers and the infection that caused them. I called it "poison." I was convinced that it was damaging him, hurting him permanently. I became so obssessed about it that I could hardly be in the room during the time that the "black bag" was hanging there.

And still, Daniel watched TV. He listened to his music. He ordered movies and we all watched them in the evening. I read to him. The sun came in his window every day. He went out of his room to physical therapy, outside in the garden, to the activities room. He "talked" on the phone with friends and family, making one noise for no, two for yes. He seemed less withdrawn, less depressed, and he talked with the techs who were still assigned to him, twenty-four hours a day, for he had never been able to learn to operate the calling devices.

One day, Susan called. She was crying. She had gone to the obstetrician for blood tests. They had discovered a blood platelet count so low that she was being admitted to the hospital immediately. They were not sure that she could keep the pregnancy.

"I have to go there," Leonard said, who had just arrived himself in Denver.

"My baby," I cried. "I want to go."

"No, Daniel needs you here. Besides, I have to go and talk to the doctors. I have to see for myself what's happening."

"You're right, I guess."

"Look up," Leonard said. "Do you see that black star? It's hanging over us. It won't ever go away."

I cried and cried. And got him a plane reservation. And took him to the airport and put him on the plane to Los Angeles, and Susan.

This was to have been a family reunion weekend. Susan and Debbie were to have come from Los Angeles to Denver. Leonard was here. We were all to have been together. We had been looking forward to it for weeks. Now, there was to be no weekend of family. Instead, there was just more worry, more tears.

Debbie decided to come anyway. I was afraid to let her. With two children in the hospital very ill, I was afraid to risk the third in any way. Finally, she convinced me.

We came from the airport to find Daniel in physical therapy, having a test of his ability to move and feel. I was happy that more tests were being done, but Daniel was not. And he didn't want me there.

While we had shared so much, I had been aware for a while that Daniel was not always telling me everything he knew about his condition. Sometimes, he avoided telling me things, I thought. I kept my dreams and ideals. He knew otherwise, and had lost hope, but didn't want to take it away from me. I became poignantly aware of this as I sat with Debbie, newly arrived, to watch him be tested. He tried to turn his head away. At times, he looked at me and I could so clearly read his eyes. Go away, he was saying silently, don't watch this. I don't want you to see. I don't want you to know. I know it's much worse than you imagine. I don't want you to be hurt, or to suffer. Go away.

He was right. I didn't want to know. I wanted to keep positive thoughts and plans. I took Debbie, and went away.

A visit to Craig had been scheduled for our whole family that day. Now, Leonard and Susan were not here. Daniel didn't want to wait, and we decided to go anyway.

With the social worker, we visited the lobby, and then went up to the physical therapy area. We looked at all the equipment, and the patients using it. I asked specifically what equipment there would be for Daniel to use. Despite all the words of encouragement in which the answer was couched, I determined that he would not be able to use much. We went on, to the car without wheels, where people learned to transfer and, if appropriate, to drive. Again, this would never be for Daniel. We went on to see the swimming pool, where patients could go for exercise and strengthening. Daniel would not be using that, either. We went to see the gym, with a beautiful basketball court where wheelchair sports were played. Again, not for Daniel.

We were shown a variety of wheelchairs. Daniel's would be the biggest and heaviest, a sip-and-puff. It did not seem that he would even be able to operate one with head controls, due to the extent of his injuries. We looked at the quad tubs. I don't know why, but they depressed and upset me terribly. Quad tubs are shallow pans, placed at waist level for the caregiver, on two columns. This would be the only kind of "bath" Daniel would ever be able to take.

We looked at patient's rooms. Most were two bedded, with posters, pictures, TVs, audio equipment. They looked warm and inviting and private, like a college dorm room. But these, too, would not be for Daniel, and we were taken to see a four-bedded room for ventilator patients. The social worker explained that it was easier to have them all together, so that they could better be monitored. The room was dark, noisy, crowded, and completely and totally unprivate. I shivered to myself. How could he stay here? How could he sleep?

After a visit to Craig's outdoor area, where Daniel could sit in the sun, we returned to his room in neurotrauma. We were all very quiet. I felt as though we could not share our thoughts, for they were too sad, too depressing, to share. Neither Debbie nor Daniel nor I were willing to take the first step and share our impressions. Craig had everything to offer. But what it could offer Daniel was minimal. I think we were all thinking the same thoughts: that there was very little, if any, real rehabilitation possible if Daniel continued to remain where he was neurologically.

Finally, I broached the subject with Daniel. We did not talk about rehabilitation. Instead, we focussed on something much easier: the room. We agreed that Daniel would be very unhappy in a four-bedded room, and that we would try to request that he be placed in a two-bedded one. When I did make that request, it was accepted and I was told that arrangments could possibly be made, depending on availability. That seemed, in our position, already a wonderful accomplishment.

Debbie left, and Leonard came back. Susan's platelet count was under control, and a plan for her care had been made. I did not tell him about Craig and what I had realized. I wanted to shield him, as Daniel shielded me.

Finally, Daniel was given the swallow test, and a film was made of him eating a spoonful of pudding. I was not there, but Leonard told me that they stopped the test with the first trial. Daniel had failed. He had aspirated that small spoonful of pudding. We asked that the film be brought to Daniel's room and, together, watched the pudding hesitate, them go into his trachea instead of his esophagus. With that brief moment went all my hopes of Daniel's being able to eat and drink, at least for the present. I still had hopes that he would improve, or be taught swallowing techniques, or something, so that he could eat and drink. The speech pathologist was supportive: she would try to work with him, she promised, and see what could be done.

A much more poignant disappointment came soon after. A respiratory technician told us excitely that Daniel was beginning to breathe on his own! She showed us a little green light on the ventilator which indicated Daniel's effort. I was ecstatic.

I could not take my eyes off the machine. Sure enough, with each breath, the little green light came on!

We told Daniel, expecting great enthusiasm. Instead, he greeted the great news in silence. I think *he* knew that nothing had changed, no matter what the machine said. We called Dr. P. He came, and stood quietly by the bed. He looked down at Daniel for a long time, but said nothing. Then he went out, asking that the tubing be changed, and that he be called again if the green light was still coming on. The tubing was changed. The green light went out. The disappointment was like a punch in the stomach. It took my breath away.

Still, there were the good things. Daniel was out of bed daily. He was reading at my insistence, with a special device to hold magazines. He talked to us and to his friends and to the techs. He seemed a bit more in control of what was going on, at least from the point of view of his daily routine and care. The sun was still shining, and there was still hope.

I had planned to try to teach my classes and return to work, shuttling back and forth to Denver weekly or biweekly. As the time for leaving approached, I became terribly sad. I simply did not want to leave Daniel. I reasoned with myself about it all the time. I told myself, first and most importantly, that he needed to realize that he could survive by himself, could get his needs met on his own. He needed to know that he could be independent. It was not good for him to rely on me too much. Then, I told myself that I needed to maintain some contact with my own life. I had interrupted my teaching in the summer. I was scheduled for two classes in the fall. I felt I owed it to the schools, and to my consulting jobs, to return to my responsibilities.

I had not left Daniel since the accident. I had been his mouth and hands, his advocate, his friend, his mother. This would be, for me, one of the hardest moments.

I tried to prepare us both. I made a large chart, with everyone's vistation schedules: mine and Leonard's and Susan's and Debbie's and his grandmother's and his uncle's and his friends'.

I hung it on the wall where he could see it. I also wrote a letter for the techs who would be taking care of them.

"I have not left Daniel since his accident, but I must leave him now. I am leaving my precious son in your keeping," I wrote, "please take care of him. I know you are busy, but please take care of him."

"Please talk to him. He needs the stimulation of good conversation."

"Put the special balm on his hands and feet."

"Make sure he reads every day."

"Encourage him to get up, even when he says he doesn't want to. He needs to get used to being out of bed."

"Open his curtains, to help him to know day from night."

"Take him outside, when you can. He loves to be out."

"Help him to choose what he wants to wear, to listen to, to watch on TV. Making choices is important."

I hung that on the wall as well.

Susan had her first sonogram, to see if the baby was developing normally. I hung that on the wall as well.

"Thirty-two weeks to unclehood," I wrote on the paper. It seemed so near. And yet, I wondered as I wrote, where would we all be in thirty-two weeks? Would Susan keep the pregnancy? Would Daniel have gotten some function back? Would he be finished with rehabilitation? Would he be home, in a house newly made accessible? Would he be in school?

By the nurses' station in the neurotrauma unit was a large white board. On it was listed every patient's name, and what the plans were for that patient. All Daniel's activities were listed on that board: trips outdoors, physical therapy, tests, conferences, and so on. Each day when I arrived I checked the board to see what Daniel would be doing that day. On the board, by other names, the magic words would appear: "To Craig." I would stare at them, wishing with every ounce of strength that I could see those magic words by Daniel's name. We had discussed dates, but tests, and the fever, and other complications kept him at neurotrauma. Would he ever move on? I had to know, before I left. I approached Dr. B. and he gave me a date that I could live with, hope with, and pray over. It was September 11. It was soon.

Daniel tried to take my leaving in good spirits, but I could tell he was upset. I told him all the reasons, especially that he needed to see that he could make it without me. I told him he must be sick of me hanging over him by now, but he said he wasn't. It hurt terribly to see him so upset.

He wouldn't be alone for more than two days, I reasoned with both of us. Susan was arriving then, and then his best friend from home was coming for four days. And then I would be back. That didn't seem to help either. I understood how he was feeling. I was the constant in his life thus far. And the constant was leaving.

I knew that I was leaving him in good hands: caring hands, expert hands. I was heartened by the progress he was making. Life seemed stable, and as comfortable as possible. He was settled into a good routine. But he was my baby and they had to pull me away and drag me crying from his bedside, and down the hall, and into the elevator.

14

The Gathering Clouds

DANIEL'S DAILY ACTIVITIES

Wednesday, August 26

8:00–9:00 A.M.: Bed bath.
10:00–12:00 A.M.: Gym.
2:00–2:30 P.M.: Grounds outing with Jill, respiratory, and
  technician.
2:30–around 4:00 P.M.: Sat up in gym.
  Will watch *Bugsy* tonight.
11:00 P.M.: Daniel sleeping soundly.

Thursday, August 27

12:00–7:30 A.M.: Dan slept all night.
7:30 A.M.: Dan awake.
8:30 A.M.: Gave him a bath.
10:00 A.M.: Dan got up in wheelchair and went to the gym.
12:00 P.M.: Came back from gym pretty tired. He's getting up at
  1 P.M. to go on an outing with Jill.
1:30–2:15 P.M.: Grounds outing with Jill and the respiratory
  technician.
  Dan is enjoying getting out.
  Introduced him to the " ? Reader."
  Will sit him up this evening.
  Opened cards.
3:30 P.M.: Daniel returned from gym. We put Daniel to bed,

gave him a bed bath, brushed his teeth and took off his clothes. Bag balm (to hands and feet to prevent dry cracked skin), tracheotomy dressing change.

5:00 P.M.: Dan watched TV until 9 P.M. Debbie called around 7:30 P.M.

9:00 P.M.: Gave Daniel bowel program with good results.

9:30 P.M.: Daniel watched *Bugsy* until 11:30 P.M.

11:30–12 A.M.: Daniel received respiratory treatments and went to sleep.

Friday, August 28

12:30 A.M.: Daniel is sleeping soundly. Daniel slept with little or no interruption throughout the night.

7:00 A.M.: Morning cares, prep for getting up in the gym.

10:00 A.M.: Up in gym.
   Used adaptive equipment for reading *Life* magazine.
   Read his mail and four cards today.

12:00 P.M.: Back in bed for a lunch time snooze

1:45 P.M.: Dan went back to the gym where Jill and recreational therapy is setting him up with an activity.

3:00 P.M.: Randy the sitter leaves and Andreas takes over.

3:30 P.M.: Dan went back to bed. Sam is his sitter. Rested and then wanted to watch TV. Turned TV on at about 4:30. Bronco's game came on at 7:00. Dan watched until half time. Susan came so Dan had the TV cut off so he could visit with Susan (time 8:30). At 9:15 started watching *King Ralph*. Dan has had trouble breathing tonight.

Saturday, August 29

11:00 P.M.–7:00 A.M.: Daniel is experiencing shortness of breath. Frank from respiratory is trying to locate the problem. We hooked him up to a pulse oxygen to see his oxygen blood level. Oxygen level is OK. Suction and treatment is required. Also, Dan has a temp of 38.7 and we are working on this to control it. Daniel's pain level is OK as of 11 P.M. Daniel went to sleep at 12:30 A.M. Susan's phone # is 789-0953.

7:00 A.M.–3:00 P.M.: Daniel has been awake since 6:30 A.M. and can't go back to sleep. He seems to be in pain so I'm waiting until his pain medication to begin his cares. Also, his temp is at 39, so we will be addressing this. Temp started dropping at around 7:50 A.M.and we will be dressing him at 8:00 A.M. Daniel got a complete bed bath at 8:30 and requested to sleep until 10:00 A.M. and get dressed and up by 10:30. From 10:30 to 12:00 Daniel rested due to his lack of sleep at night. Susan has been here most of the day. She did his nails. Jill is going to demonstrate a reading adaptation device.

3:00 P.M.–11:00 P.M.: Dan is constantly requesting pain medication. He refused to get up. Dan got his pain medication at

5:00 P.M. and went to sleep immediately after that. He slept from about 5:15 to 7:30 P.M. and immediately requested pain medication. Dan's nurse gave him his pain meds at 8:00 P.M. I did his trach cares, put bag balm on his hands and feet, and all his H.S. care.

Sunday, August 30

11:00 P.M.–7:00 A.M.: Daniel slept most of the night. He was less anxious during the night as he was during the day. He became more anxious at around 4:00 A.M. complaining of shortness of breath. Nurses and respiratory are aware of his shortness of breath.

7:00 A.M.–3:00 P.M.: Daniel was anxious this A.M. Didn't sleep well last night. Asking for pain meds continually, and complaining of shortness of breath. I called respiratory who responded shortly but his anxiety continued. At 12:00 noon he was resting peacefully. Slept for approx. 1 hour.

3:00 P.M.–11:00 P.M.: Dan went to nuclear medicine at 3:30. He did not have much fun there, had some problems with ventilator when hooked up to what I call glow juice. We bagged him through the test. Dan had friends from school come and see him. Dan got some rest on and off most all evening. At about 9:00 I took Teds (elastic stockings) off and discovered right leg much larger than left, leg measurements were taken and doctor was called. NEVA came and did their tests, possible blood clots. Dan listened to some music and had a bath and when I left (11:30) was going to watch *Medicine Man* (a movie).

Monday, August 31

7:00 A.M.–3:00 P.M.: Daniel is having a much better day than yesterday. He is catching up on some "Z's" after missing so much sleep through the weekend. Unfortunately, he is on bed rest today due to the possiblity of a blood clot in his right leg. NEVA is due to arrive anytime this morning and locate the clot. All in all he is just really tired and has slept on and off through the shift.

3:00 P.M.–11:00 P.M.: Dan is having a much better day. Friends Steve and sister were here to see him. Dan is on bedrest so I will keep him busy tonight with books, music, movies. Dan got a shave, and after shave, hair wash, and bath, and he now looks much better and feels better too. Seems to be resting better too.

Tuesday, September 1

8:15: Mother called. Geraldine from "Life Line" was his sitter for today. Had agreed to bed bath, went down for a treatment, had a hard time, came back doing fair. Temp has been up. Put ice pack on. Have a good night.

Have a good night. And so, the record ends.

Dan's daily activities were kept for me by the technicians and sitters who cared for him during the days that I was away. I called constantly, for I was not at peace away from Daniel. I called the techs, the nurses, the doctor, and, most of all, of course, Daniel.

I told him about home, about our dogs: Josie getting senile and old, Wilmington and his stick, and Jamaica and her really being a person. I told him about our sailboat that had sunk while I was gone, and about the nice neighbors who refloated it. I told him about the garden, his room, his car. I told him about people he knew and places he loved. He answered with his special noises. One for yes and two for no and several for I don't know. I tried to be cheerful and positive but running through these days was a sense of irreality. I knew, somehow, that the good days wouldn't hold.

Not that even the good days were "good" by any standard Daniel had known. "Going to gym" sounded great, but one must remember that this consisted of sitting at about a thirty-degree angle only in a room which had equipment which he couldn't use, staring at a fish tank for an hour or so. "Outings" were brief trips to the grounds of the hospital, with two or three attendants. Three people were required to put Daniel in a wheelchair, always in a semi-reclining position. They had to tie his hands together to transfer him, because otherwise they would fall limply and insensately down toward the ground. A "reading activity" consisted of a special adaptive device which could hold a magazine over his head. Someone else turned the pages, and adjusted the device, which inevitably covered lines of the reading material. He was not eating or drinking. "A lunchtime snooze" was possible to someone who was being fed by continuous intravenous feedings.

I do not mean in any way to devalue the programs or activities which were provided at neurotrauma through Craig. They were wonderful, and it was particularly wonderful to see how much time and effort and patience was put into the care of one person, to try to make life as pleasant as possible for him. But always there was the knowledge that it would not improve. It would always require this much effort for Daniel to do anything at all. Effort on the part of caregivers, for Daniel himself could make no effort in his own behalf.

Daniel continued to be on large amounts of medications. He still took "poison," and various pain medication, blood medications, infection medications, breathing medications for his lungs, and others I can't even recall. He alternated between pain and drowsiness from drugs.

Susan's reports from the days she spent with Daniel were very discouraging. She said he was always agitated, in pain and suffering, or asleep from the drugs. She said that he constantly asked for pain medications before the required number of hours had elapsed, and begged and begged the nurses. She said he was very uncomfortable all the time from breathing problems, and that suctioning was painful and very frequent.

Dear Daniel,

It's Sunday night and I am getting your mail ready to send to you, so I thought I'd write you some mail of my own. I have been very upset all day with how sick you have been. I have been calling the hospital constantly and Dad says I have to stop because I will make a nuisance of myself. I know it's true but it's so hard for me not to be right there and to see for myself how you are. Susan paints a gloomy picture, and she, too, is very upset with how badly you feel.

I don't understand what happened. At first we got glowing reports of Dan, up in the wheelchair twice a day, Dan outside, Dan reading, Dan going longer with no meds. And then all of a sudden the bottom falls out of the world again and it's Dan, really sick and back on the big ventilator and needing oxygen and transfusions.

In school of social work we learned that it's forward, then back again, then forward, the back. The backs are not as far back as the first ones—each is a little less back. I always think about that with you—we've had so many forwards and backs. But, hopefully, each back hasn't been as far back, or for very long. I hope that, by the time you get this letter, you're on a forward track again, and feel better and stronger.

We're trying to hold down the home front here. We had a tornado, if you can believe it, in Glen Burnie the other day. We got very high winds and it was really scary. I was, of course, home alone as Dad was on call. The wind blew so that the power went out, and stayed out for several hours. It was late afternoon and I was scared it was going to get dark. I closed all the curtains in case a window blew in and when I got to the library, Wilmington was sitting on my brand new, powder-blue-and-white couch that I got just before your accident, and that I've hardly sat on yet! I tried to yell at him but he wouldn't move. Finally, I pulled him off—and he climbed right back on. He was shaking so hard with terror that you could see it through his fur. I sat on the couch with him curled up by me. I was kind of scared, myself. Odie and Mayda sat right nearby, too. Then just as it was getting dark, the lights went back on. Some neighbors I don't really know (new people in the big white house) who offered to watch our boats came to check on them after the tornado. It was nice of them. We never check the boats after a storm, do we? We just assume they will be OK.

Friday night we went to services. We're meeting in a church temporarily (again) as the building is being rebuilt. Wait till you see it! It will be ready for the high holidays. The carpet is maroon and the bima is blue and the chairs as a rose/maroon color. There's even air conditioning. We already got new members and the new schoolrooms are already too small, so we have to make some changes and additions already.

Peggy and Harvey and Dad and I went to dinner at the Calvert House—not yours; this is a restaurant on Route 2 right near Parole. We had fish for dinner and I told them how Rona was going to get Patrick to send you some shrimp and soft shell crabs as soon as you can eat again. I hope you'll like them.

Saturday I had lunch with a friend and then I went to have my hair done. I got it highlighted so it's lighter and she trimmed it a little. Do you remember Kay, the hairdresser from Susan's wedding? That's who I went to. Then I went to the grocery store. I still have your list of groceries on the little piece of paper in my sun visor. Remember? It was the last list you made for me before you went away to college. It says: spaghettios, hot dogs and buns, ketchup, hot pockets, and a few other things. I'm still saving it.

Saturday night we went out with the Cochrans. First they came over for a while and we played with Wilmington, throwing sticks for him into the creek. He loved all the attention. He gets so alert and involved. Do you remember how hard he can concentrate on a stick? How he looks at you? He's really just like a person. Odie and Mayda just sat around and watched, of course. Willie got tired after a while and saved face, as he usually does, by sitting down and eating some of the stick. After a few minutes, he was back for more! We went to Chili's and I remembered the night of nights—the night you got into Rochester Early Decision and you and Dad met me there with the letter hidden in another letter. Remember how excited we all were? I always look at the place we sat and, if it's empty, request it. But it was full and so we sat elsewhere.

Dad has been out attacking the bushes this weekend. The weeds are out of this world awful. Guess you won't have to worry about being asked to weed in the near future! I weeded my little garden in the back and Dad began with the front. Then he got the hedge clippers and bush trimmers. He chopped away at all the bushes. Then he got wilder and wilder. He actually cut down the cherry tree—the one near the front walk, and also the miniature Japanese something or other in front of the electric meter. Not content with that, he cut our a triangle of the scrunchy bushes on the lowest level by the walk, you know, those on the right. He started to take out pieces of railroad tie wall. He wants grass to curve up that level, near the walk. He says he cut down the trees because they were blocking his view of the garden. The years come and the years go, but your Dad stays the same. Turn him loose with a sharp implement, and he'll find a find a tree to cut down.

It looks so bare out front without the two trees and the bushes by the walk. I wonder when he plans to plant the grass?

Of course, does he cut down the trees he needs to cut down, the ones on the water side that block my view? No. They are farther down the list. They require that he put on winter clothes so he won't get hurt by all the pricker bushes. So my view is blocked where I want it to be, and I have a view where I didn't need one. We had our usual arguments over this. You know how we get.

I got my stuff ready for the two courses I'm teaching —ethics at Catholic University for social workers, and straight ethics at the community college. It's a whole lot easier when you've taught the course before but I changed it because I wanted to include a modern American woman ethicist named Sisela Bok. She wrote a book called *Lying* in which she discusses "lying in public and private life." I thought it would be fun to have a contemporary writer, and that the students would enjoy integrating some modern moral problems in with their Aristotle and Kant. Not that I don't, as you know, adore Aristotle especially, but just that we have so many ethical problems in our society that could use some thoughtful discussion and reflection. And since mine always are seminar classes, I think it gives the students something immediate to relate to.

We're still eating things that people brought to us and left in the refrigerator and freezer. They brought really good stuff. I know you don't remember this, but there's a very special gourmet ice cream store in Rome, near the Pantheon, called Giolitti's. One of the relatives came to America and opened a restaurant on Main street called La Piccola Roma. We went there and it was very good but also very expensive so we haven't gone back. Anyhow, now they opened a Giolitti's Deli near the Sears Automotive store. They have the best Italian things there—right from Rome. Anyhow, the stuff people brought us is all from this Giolitti's. It's wonderful. Tomorrow I'm having lunch there with Joanne Richard, Lance's mother. She wanted to talk with me and be supportive. But to me Lance, five years post accident, is not too much like you at this point. I hope in five years you'll be just like him! A Craig graduate, happy, out in the world. He lives in Miami and he and his girlfriend had to evacuate from the hurricane and move inland for the duration.

How is your schoolwork? Did you have to stop even thinking about it because you were so sick? I hope you will get to it soon. May I ask Les how it is going?

Remember that you are in our thoughts with love all day and all night. I even dream about you. I am with you in Denver in spirit, cheering you on and wishing you well and sending love and support. I'll write more soon.

Love,
Mom

Though I tried very hard to pick up the lost threads of a splintered lifetime, I could not take my mind from Daniel, even for minutes at a time. I tried to go to work, to see friends, to take care of my house. Somehow I did these things. Somehow, for my mind and heart were in Denver.

Finally, on Wednesday, September 2, Daniel's doctor called. Daniel had been taken to x-ray for something. In the elevator, on the way to x-ray, he had an accident somehow, and lost conciousness. They had revived him, but Daniel and the staff were both shaken badly. His doctor thought he would need to transfer him to the ICU again. He told me perhaps I had better come. Dan was having serious problems. He had emboli which could shift and cause a painful death at any time. His respiratory situation was precarious. His fevers were still uncontrolled.

I reached Daniel long before my letter.

In Denver, the sun was still shining. But for me, the dark clouds, always on the horizon, had gathered. They were moving ever closer. Nonetheless, as my plane arrived, I could only be happy, in a strange way. I felt better when I was with Daniel. I didn't want to leave him. I was glad to be back. I even had an apartment in my old building back. Home had felt alien. It was almost as though being with Daniel in Denver was the normal, and being home the abnormal.

It was as though I had never left him, for the routine picked up where it had left off. I was with Daniel all day, and many nights, which at first created a problem with the ICU. Because of Daniel's fears of being alone with the ventilator, based, I thought, on several very real incidents where the tubing had become unhooked, the unheard-of was done for him: he was allowed a sitter in the ICU. This sitter was arranged early in the day for the evening, when, presumably, I would leave to return to the apartment for the night.

However, there were many nights that I never left. Daniel preferred me to stay, and I preferred to be with him. So, every evening, my body had a war with my mind and emotions. I need rest, my body would argue. I need to lie flat, on a mattress. But I love him, my emotions would answer, and I don't want to be away from him for a moment. And besides, my mind would join in, who knows what can happen? Who can take care of a son better than a mother? Can a stranger from an agency? Usu-ally, my mind and emotions won, but sometimes the battle raged until the last minute. Then, I would ask the nurse to can-cel the sitter. I did not stop to think, in my distress, what this did to the sitter's schedule. After the first few times, it was brought to my attention, and the decision was made earlier in the day. Always, Daniel participated in it. He clearly wanted me to stay, and it was not often that he willingly sent me home.

In the ICU I slept in a visitor chair, with my feet up on another visitor chair. I tried to sleep as close to Daniel as possi-ble, pushing the chairs up against his bed. I took my pillows and blankets and curled up, leaning my head against his bed. I found a great deal of comfort in this nearness, for it seemed to me sometimes that Daniel and I were all alone in the world, a silent, dark world of monitors and machines and soft footsteps in the distance. I didn't have to "guard" the monitors here. I had only to respond to his needs, when he made his noise to get my attention: to suction his mouth, to turn his head, to scratch his nose, to call for the nurse or the respiratory technician.

"I'm so dependent, Mom," Dan would mouth at me. "I hate being dependent upon all these people all the time. I'm so helpless."

"You're not helpless," I answered forcefully. "Not as long as I'm here you're not."

Dan looked at me sadly, and did not answer. It was only then that I thought about what I had said. Having me act in his behalf was still being helpless to a red-blooded twenty-one-year-old young man. My comment, well-meant, might only have increased his feelings of dependence. The dependence itself, though, was real, and no words or phrases or thoughts could deny or sugar-coat that fact.

After a few days, Leonard joined me in Denver. Daniel was stable, though the doctors wanted him to remain in the ICU. He was stable, but at a level that was unbearable to him. He continued to ask for pain medication, and it was hard for me to separate his actual physical pain from his psychological pain.

Sometimes it seemed the medicine was to ease the psychological as much, at least, as the physical.

Daniel had developed ARDS, Adult Respiratory Distress Syndrome. His lungs could not expand even with the air that the ventilator pushed in them. They were stiff. Each day, Dr. P. would adjust the ventilator settings to try to compensate for the inelasticity. Each day, the pressure in Daniel's stiff lungs crept higher and higher. Bit by bit, his respiratory condition deteriorated. I always watched the monitor, watched the constantly changing numbers that indicated my child's ability to take in air. I became obsessed with it. Not to stress Daniel further, I tried to watch surreptitiously, my eyes always drawn in silence to the pattern of numbers on the dark face of the ventilator. Those numbers seemed to slowly become more and more important. I knew ARDS caused death in its severe form. The threat was still far, far away. However, this too was a slowly growing black spot on the horizon.

My brother came to visit for the weekend also. He had not seen Daniel since the accident, and I tried to allow them some space, sitting and reading in the waiting room instead of staying with Daniel. I talked with random people. Everyone was pleasant but preoccupied with their own problems and there was not the esprit de corps of the dirty green waiting room in Rochester. I had not noticed because I had not spent any time in the waiting room before. I missed the closeness of my ICU family very much.

On Monday afternoon Leonard convinced me to try to go home. My classes started Wednesday evening, and I had to prepare myself. If I wanted to try to keep my own life together, I needed to be able to leave. I was in a torment. I didn't want to leave my child, but I also knew that, no matter what happened, I would need a life of my own to which to return. My brother was to stay through Tuesday, and I would be back on Friday. Daniel did not insist that I stay. He seemed to understand the reasons for my leaving, but it broke my heart, still, to walk out of that room and down the hall, away from him.

I was silent through the flight home. I was silent at home the next day. Desperately, I began to prepare for my classes, calling Denver every two to three hours for reports on the ventilator settings. I could not sleep that night, calling through the night. The next day was Wednesday, Leonard's surgery day, the day of the week when he was completely unreachable.

I continued to call for the ventilator numbers. They were getting worse. Unable to function at home, out of my mind with worry, I took a big step. I called and cancelled my teaching for the semester. I cancelled my consulting. I changed my appointments and my life. I could not stay in Annapolis. I was moving to Denver, to stay there as long as Daniel was there. What happened to my own life was inconsequential, trivial in comparison with my need to be with Daniel, and, I believed, Daniel's need to have me there to care for and coddle and support him. I called once again, and told the nurse to tell Daniel I was on my way, and that I would never, never leave him again.

15

I Am Leaving Home the Mother of Three, and Will Return the Mother of Two

In less time than I would have believed possible, I was ready. When it's *really* an emergency, I noticed with some detachment, one can be prepared in just minutes. I was ready much sooner than the flight would be. Alone and waiting, I looked around my home.

Everything was silent and still. The sun shone on the bedroom rug, making a sharp line between light and shadow. I stared at it for a long moment. It seemed to me like a line between life and death, between the known and the unknown. How could I prepare myself for what was ahead? How could I be strong, if I needed to help my child across the line? How would it be, to be on one side of the line while my beloved Daniel was on the other?

I walked down the hall to his room, and opened the door. The juxtaposition between Daniel's room, with his wall of playing cards from around the world, his bed with his favorite quilt, his alarm clock still keeping the time, his posters, his desk and favorite chair, and the reality of Denver, seemed more than my mind could absorb. His sports trophies glinted in the sunshine, from the earliest kiddie league to Severn's most valuable player award. There would never be another, I thought. Still, even at that moment, I was proud of the wonderful moments I remembered of Daniel and sports, proud of his achievements. His typewriter was sticking partly out from under his bed. It had been abandoned with college, when he had invested in an computer. His shelves were filled with all the special mementos of a young man's life: glasses from proms, mugs from fraternity parties, childhood souvenirs from trips, pictures of his sisters, a stuffed sheep toy, a tarantula mounted in a glass box. Dusty, familiar. His room smelled of him.

I finally looked at the pile of boxes and clothes at one corner: all the things that Leonard had brought home from the University of Rochester that desperate day. No one had unpacked them yet. They were here, waiting for the hand of their owner. The hand that, I knew, would never touch them again. I imagined him home, unpacking after the year of school, setting up his stereo, and blasting Grateful Dead tunes through the house. I imagined the gigantic pile of laundry he always had with him. Do all boys, I wondered, come home with duffel bags full of dirty laundry? I suspected that many did. I knew I would never wash this laundry, though. I would want to preserve it, dirty from his games, studies, and parties. Dirty with happy memories.

I walked out of his room and closed the door behind me, closing off all the familiar things. What was going to be with Daniel, I knew, was not going to be familiar. It would be another whole world, for us both, for all of us who loved him.

I went outside and sat on the deck and looked out at the water. The sun was shining, and it was one of those perfect days at the end of summer. Too perfect. Tears came, then, as I thought that summer was ending, and that perhaps Daniel's life was ending also. The season of death was upon us, it seemed to me as I looked out at this last, lingering day, which I had begun with hope, and which was ending in sadness.

I wanted to bring Daniel home. If he was going to die, I wanted him to die at home, with all of his things around him: his dogs, his house and deck and stereo and his friends from home. I wanted to bring him home to rest and safety, for isn't home the place where we are always safe, where we can always rest? I wanted to take care of him myself. I wanted him away from the world of the hospital. And all the while that I was wanting and wishing, I knew that Daniel would never, never, never come home again. He was connected to the hospital by lifelines that could never be suspended or broken. He was more dependent upon the hospital for life support than ever.

I swung my legs out over the steep drop down to the water from the deck. Is this really happening, I asked myself for the millionth time? Am I really sitting here waiting to go to the airport, hoping Daniel is still alive by the time I reach Denver?

At last, my friend arrived to take me to the airport. As we drove out of the driveway, I turned back and said goodbye for the last time to home as I knew it.

"I'm leaving home the mother of three," I told my friend, "and I will return the mother of two."

My friend didn't try to deny this. She knew better.

Alone at the airport, I tried again to reach Leonard, Susan, Debbie. I could find no one. I called Swedish. Daniel was still alive. He was waiting for me.

And then, there was trouble with the flight. I was scheduled Baltimore to O'Hare, then O'Hare to Denver. The plane from Baltimore was late. I could miss my connection. I could, instead, wait several hours at the airport, then catch a direct flight. The airline personnel shared my agony, and tried to help me. The reservation agent I had gotten to know, in Chicago, spoke with me, as did the local agents. I was crying, and everyone was trying to help, but planes and airports do not easily lend themselves to sympathy for individuals. Finally, I chose to board the plane to O'Hare. I had to be on my way. I needed to feel that I was getting a little closer to Daniel. Halfway was better than no way.

The agents accompanied me on board. They had given me a seat in first class. I sank into the unaccustomed luxury gratefully, but thought that it would have been nice to have this special treat for a happy reason, rather than a tragic one.

I cried silently during much of the flight. There was a man sitting next to me, studiously avoiding looking in my direction. Finally, he asked:

"Can I get you the stewardess? Do you need anything?"

"No," I answered through my tears, "I'm just trying to get to my son. He had an accident, and he's dying in Denver."

"Oh."

We rode a while in silence.

I watched the man begin to try to use the on-board phone at our seat. He kept trying to spring it, but it was stuck. Finally, he worked it free. He dialed a number. Helpless, I had no choice but to listen.

"Hi, Chris," he said, "I just thought I'd call and say hello. I'm flying out to Chicago."

"Yes, on business. I'll be there for three days. How's Barbara?"

"That's good. And the kids?"

"Great. Is Brad playing baseball this season?"

"How's he doing?"

"And how are you doing? How's work going?"

"That's fine. It sounds like you've got everything under control at that end."

"Well, that's all. I haven't spoken to you in a long time, I know. I just thought I'd call and say hello."

"And son, take care of yourself. I just wanted to say I love you."

He hung up, picked up his paper, and proceded to ignore me the rest of the flight. I sat and stared out of the window at the approaching darkness of the night sky.

At O'Hare the ticketing agent had tracked my flight. She had personally come to the airport, seen that I had missed my connection, gotten me a boarding pass for the next plane to Denver, and arranged to spend the intervening time with me to help me. I was, and always will be, so grateful for her kindness, far above and beyond any possible responsibility she might have had. How different, I thought, from the man on the plane. I shivered as I poured out my grief into sympathetic though unknown ears.

I called Denver again.

"Tell him I'm on my way," I begged the nurse. "Tell him the plane was late. Tell him I'm coming as fast as I can."

From the plane, I finally watched the lights of Denver appear, blinking in the dark sky. One of those lights, I thought, could be the hospital. Hold on Dan, I whispered to myself, I'm almost here.

My heart was pounding and it seemed to me one unbroken motion: getting off the plane and walking to the taxi stand and the long ride to Swedish and the inane conversation with the taxi driver and walking to the elevator and going up and down the hall to intensive care and to his room and in. And then I took another breath. We were together. We were safe.

I started to cry. He was lying there, with the usual multitude of tubes and wires and monitors attached, the ventilator hissing and clicking, the feeding tube dripping. He could not turn his head to see me. He could not touch me. But he was alive, warm, wide awake and waiting for me and happy to see me.

I slid my overnight case into a corner, went to Daniel and hugged him tightly even though I knew he couldn't feel my hug. I could feel it. I didn't even care if my hair touched his face even though I knew that made him mad. I was so glad to be with him. I loved him so.

"I'm here, Dan," I said. "I'm here. You know, sick boys need their moms. And I'm yours. And no matter what happens, I'm never going to leave you again. Never, never. I'm not going home, I'm not going to work, I'm moving to Denver and staying with you forever."

He smiled at me. And I believe that this made him as happy and secure as, under the circumstances, he could be.

16

Thirty Percent Is Not Much Chance

All night, that first night back, I watched Daniel's ventilator. I slept in fits and starts and snatches. The numbers would be stable for a while, and then shoot up terrifyingly, indicating a potentially lethal increase in pressure in his lungs.

I never did truly understand all the numbers and gauges, but I struggled to grasp, with my layman's knowledge, what was happening in Daniel's chest. It seemed that his lungs could expand less and less, had less and less elasticity, and that more and more pressure was needed to get sufficient air into his system. As the numbers went higher and higher, creeping steadily toward the point where they could not be adjusted further, I watched him fearfully. I was afraid his lungs would burst from the pressure. I was afraid he would have terrible pain from the pressure. I was afraid he would die from the pressure. I was afraid, very afraid, and through the night I tried to look casually and inconspicuously at the numbers, tried to conceal from him the fear that I felt.

During the early morning hours, as I was watching, his ventilator tubing popped off from the machine. Quickly, my heart lurching in terror, I reached over and reconnected it, then ran to get the nurse. The alarm had not gone off.

"How could this happen?," I asked, the incident validating, for me, my need to be with him every second.

"It's the pressure. When the ventilator delivers so much pressure to lungs that are inelastic, sometimes it causes the tubing to pop off."

"What are we going to do? Can't you connect it better?"

"I'll call respiratory. But don't worry. The system would have alarmed. You just got to it before it had a chance to react."

The respirator technician came to inspect the problem. He brought tubing clamps and clamped each tube securely to the machine, and to Daniel's tracheotomy site. To reassure me further, he and the nurse brought another alarm, and attached it to the ventilator. With a long extension cord, they set the alarm on a chair, outside of his room, to go off in the nurse's station area if there were any problems.

Asking for the truth about Daniel's new problems, from Daniel's pulmonary specialist, took all the strength that I had. But I had to know. I met him outside of Daniel's room.

"As you know," he said, "Daniel has Adult Respiratory Distress Syndrome. I'm not sure why this happened."

"But what does that mean?"

"It means that his lungs are stiff. They don't expand as they should. It could take a while to resolve this. And there's a definite possibility that it will not resolve."

"What does that mean? Will he die?"

"It doesn't look very good right now. He may not make it."

"What are his chances?"

"I'd say about 30 percent."

"Thirty percent? Only 30 percent? You mean there's a greater than 50–50 chance that he *won't* make it through this?"

"That's what I'd say right now."

"What are we going to do?"

"Well, we'll give it the very best we can. We'll work with the ventilator settings and keep adjusting them."

"How long before we know?"

"Hard to tell. A few days to a week, probably."

With parting words of comfort and support, he went in to Daniel. I slumped against the planter that bordered the nurse's station, dividing the helpers from the helpless, feeling a sense of numbness and shock throughout me. Surely, I thought, this could not be happening. Surely, there was no possibility that Daniel would die.

Die, I thought. Not be here. Be cold and stiff and gone. Not here for me to hold and hug and kiss. Not here for me to look at. Never come back again. My child, my baby.

Jumbled pieces of thought went through my head as I tried to grasp what the doctor had said. Though I had tried to grasp this idea before, I had done so only with my head, not with my heart. He really had said that Daniel could die. Actually, my rational brain said to my hysterical emotions, he said Daniel would probably die. How could he do that? What could I do? I was powerless to stop it. I was just an onlooker, a mother staring at numbers flashing on the black screen of a machine that was keeping the vital breath of life in her child. A machine that could not heal. It could only blow in air, as it was programmed to do. I couldn't make it keep him alive. I could do nothing. Nothing at all.

Without going back to Daniel's room, I went to the phones to call Leonard. I leaned against the wall for support.

"You have to come. Daniel can be dying."

"What do you mean?"

Wailing, I explained what Dr. P. had said.

"You have to come, now."

"All right. But I can't just drop everything. I have to arrange for coverage for my patients. Right now I have a couple of very sick people here."

"But your own child is dying."

"I know. I'll come as fast as I can."

"You'll have to close the practice. Maybe he will be all right, but 30 percent is not too much chance."

"You have to give me time. I have to take care of things here."

"But I'm all alone here. I'm scared. I need you."

"I have to be responsible to my patients. You have to give me until Saturday. I'll be there the day after tomorrow night. And I'll just stay as long as I need to."

"How will I manage until then?"

"I'll be right here. Call me anytime."

"You won't lock yourself up in the OR and leave me alone?"

"Just once, this afternoon. Just for a short time. Please. This patient is scheduled. She's here in the hospital. I can't just abandon her."

"Remind me, in my next life, never never to marry a doctor. When will *we* come first?"

"You do come first. But patients are depending on me. I can't just abandon them. It takes time to close a practice. I'll be there the day after tomorrow, no matter what."

I hung up the phone. My mind struggled to take it in. Daniel with his 30 percent chance, lying in that ICU room, not knowing. Me alone in Denver with the knowledge. Leonard trying to be physician, husband, and father. The girls, in Los Angeles, as yet unaware of the new dangers. I would wait to call them, I decided. Bad news could wait.

I walked into the waiting room and made a cup of tea. The aquarium had been taken apart for cleaning, and the bare and empty tank depressed me further, somehow. Idly, I wondered where the fish had been taken, and if they were comfortable. The television was on, as usual, with silent faces, mouths moving across the screen. Strangers lay sprawled on the couches or congregated in small groups, talking worriedly. A baby cried. Through the large windows, I could see that outside, the sun was shining. It was a sunny day in the world that I knew was there, but which had no relevance to me anymore.

I moved through the room as though a shell surrounded me. It made me invisible. No one could see me through it. It travelled with me as I walked, and molded around me when I sat at the end of a couch. No one could see that I was there, and no one even turned in my direction. No one could talk to me. No one did. I carried my tragedy alone in silence, and sipped my tea.

Too soon, worry and guilt overcame the invisible shell. I worried every minute that I was away from Daniel, every minute and second and nanosecond and whatever divisions came beyond that. With a jerk, I stood, and left the room. The shell around me was gone. Still, no one spoke to me.

Wearily, I went back to Daniel, gave him a smile and a big hug, and asked how he was doing. He was watching cartoons on television. I sat in my chair against his bed and stared dumbly at Woody Woodpecker going "ha ha ha HA ha," and listened to the "Looney Tunes" music playing. Looney, that's how I was feeling. Looney, and numb. Daniel had a 30 percent chance of living and Woody Woodpecker was laughing. Feeling close to hysteria, I wanted to laugh with him.

After a while, I looked surreptitiously again at the numbers on the machine. They were steady, each breath almost the same as the one before.

I'm losing my mind, I thought. There's nothing terrible happening. Everything is all right. Dr. P. must be wrong, or Daniel must be getting better. Maybe I didn't need to call Leonard. Maybe he shouldn't close the practice. Maybe I'm being an alarmist. He's always been in danger, since the accident. Dr. P. was the first to give it a name, and a number, that's all. It doesn't mean anything really different than usual is going on. Everything seemed so stable. The TV was playing and the machines were hissing and dripping and Dan was lying in his bed just as he always had since the accident.

And then the numbers on the ventilator shot up higher than ever.

17

Thirty Percent Is Too Much Chance

The numbers spiked higher and higher. Each time, the ventilator settings were adjusted. Each time, the numbers seemed controlled for a time. And, inexorably, the settings pushed closer and closer to the limit, the point beyond which no further adjustment was possible.

I did not leave Daniel's side. I even used the bathroom in the room, leaving the door ajar. I had faith in the power of guarding. After all, I had guarded Daniel for days on end, through crisis after crisis at Strong, and he was still alive. If I guarded carefully enough, I thought, I would keep him alive here, too. Vigilance and endurance, I thought, these were what was required of me. And, through the long hours of night and the day that was indistinguishable from it in the darkened ICU room, I guarded.

Daniel wanted me near him always. Several times each day I would feel claustrophobia, mental exhaustion, and sleepiness overcome me, and an overhwelming need to step outside of the room.

"Please don't leave me, Mom," Dan would beg. "Do you have to go?"

"I'm just going down the hall to the waiting room to get some tea and some snacks from the machine," I would explain, "I promise I'll be right back."

"When are you going to be back?"

"In ten minutes."

"Hurry up. Please come back."

I always took less than the ten minutes. I always came rushing back, knowing that Daniel felt more secure and comfortable in my presence.

Miraculously, by Saturday, the numbers seemed a little more stable. Daniel seemed to be holding his own. Maybe, I thought, his chances were getting better. Maybe he would live. I would stay here with him and guard him, and he would live and go on to Craig.

All of a sudden, feeling both joyful and trapped, I started to complain. This was the first and only time that I complained.

"I'm tired of these cartoons," I said. "My brain is rotting. Yours is too. Why can't we watch something educational? Why can't we know what's going on in the world? I'm going crazy. And so are you."

"I do know what's going on in the world," Daniel pointed out. "I watch the news every day. You know I do. You just don't watch it because you never watch the news. It's you that doesn't know anything. I do know."

And he proceded to give me examples proving his statement!

"Well, I think I just have to do something. I have to write. I need to be near my computer."

"I know."

"I'll get Dad to get me a laptop. If I'm going to be here for a long time, I need to be able to write. And we can work on your course together."

"Mom, I can't do the course."

"Maybe not now. But I need a computer anyhow, for me. I think I'm having a computer deprivation emergency."

"So call Dad. I'm sure he'll get you one."

Leonard didn't have time to get a laptop. He was busy making arrangements.

"I'm almost ready," he said Friday afternoon. "I'm keeping everyone here until I'm done. They'll just have to stay all night until I have everything together."

"Daniel's getting better, I think. I think the numbers are better."

"I better just plan to come anyway," Leonard said. "I've got it organized and I think I better just come out."

"OK I'm waiting here for you. In Daniel's room."

Slowly, ever so slowly, the hours passed, and Leonard was on the plane, and he was calling from Chicago, and from Denver airport and then, all of a sudden, he was there. Exhausted, but there.

I thought it would change things, relieve me of sole responsibility. But I was beyond change or relief. I was on my track of being with Daniel twenty-four hours a day. I was in my world where only Daniel and his immediate needs were important. I was completely integrated into Daniel's routine. There was nothing else. Leonard slept in the apartments that night. I stayed with Daniel.

Sunday afternoon, Leonard and I sat down to talk with Daniel's pulmonologist. Daniel's numbers on the ventilator were better than steady. They seemed to be improving. I was elated.

My elation was to be short-lived.

Finally, Leonard had the courage to ask the questions that I was too afraid to ask. Questions about Daniel's future.

The answers were terrifying.

Daniel would never be off the ventilator.

Daniel aspirated his own secretions.

He would therefore not be able to tolerate a "talking trach."

He would never be able to speak.

He was unable to swallow without aspirating.

He would never be able to drink.

He would never be able to eat.

His neurological level, which had ascended to almost brain stem level, would not descend. Parts of his face and head, too, had no sensation. He was unable to move anything but his eyes and mouth.

His blood clots could at any second cause painful death. If these were dissolved, new ones could easily form.

He would have continual complications: lung disease, kidney problems, fevers, infections, skin breakdown, pain, gastro-intestinal problems.

He would probably not live beyond three years, and those in very, very poor condition.

But, Dr. P. said, I was right. His lung condition was improving. The chances were that, at this point, he would survive this episode of respiratory distress.

Wave after wave of terror, and anger, swept over me. How could this be? I had brought Daniel to this place of miracles. I had guarded him through endless days and nights. I had planned and worked to give him the best future possible. But it seemed that no "best future" could be possible.

All there was ahead, for Daniel, was pain, and mental torture, and total dependence. He was marking time, until his death somewhere in the next three years, or a little beyond that.

There was nothing to hope for. Nothing to pray for. No miracles in sight, or even in the imagination.

Which agony would he suffer? A terribly painful blood clot, and rapid death? Repeated lung diseases that tortured his pulmonary system until it gave up? Fevers that would cause his face, the only part of him that could sweat, to try to relieve the burning heat, and fail? Infections that would slowly eat away at the functioning of his cells? Kidneys that stopped working?

Always with the tube in his nose for feedings. Always with the ventilator, with IVs, with chest tubes. Unable to call for help, to express a need, a wish, a hope.

No, I thought, for the first time for real. No. Not this life. Not for my son. Not for my boy who likes to run and jump and shout. Not for my boy who likes to study, to work, to party, to love, to travel, to have adventures. Not this—this death in life while all of us, himself included, watched helplessly.

Frightened of my thoughts, completely distraught, I could not return to Daniel. For the first time in a very long time, and for the last, I left him, and went with Leonard to the apartments.

Although my body collapsed immediately, I had terrible dreams. I cried and woke up, and cried more.

With the dawn, I sat and stared out of the window at the street, silent in early morning. What do I hope for, I asked myself? What *can* I hope for? Do I want my child to live, to make it through this illness? To live for *that*? Or did I want him not to make it, to die?

My mind screamed at me in silence. How can I even think of wanting my child to die? But how can I want him to live, like that? I went over and over the information that we had been given. There was no escape. No Exit, I said to myself, remembering the book by Camus or Sartre or somebody. *No Exit*. No way out. Death, or death in life.

At the hospital, I couldn't bear to be in Daniel's presence. He doesn't know, I thought. Oh, keep him from ever having to know. Protect him, shield him, do anything possible to spare him the agony of knowing what we know.

And I hugged him. I smiled. I spoke of trivialities. I watched the cartoons.

By midafternoon, meeting with the psychologist who was trying to help me cope, I had made up my mind.

"I don't know how I can do it," I sobbed, almost in a whisper. "I don't know how I can say this. But I think I want him to die. We have to turn off the ventilator. He can't live like this. It's not possible. It's not human. I *know* that he wouldn't want to do this."

"We have to help him," I said, more strongly now. "We have to take the responsibility. We are his parents. We have to let him go. We can't tell him. It would hurt him too much and I couldn't stand him to have the pain. You have to help us to let him go."

Hours later, we repeated out request to Dr. B.

"We have to let him go."

"He's as close as anyone can come to being locked in." Dr. B. said. "He can't communicate or do anything. And it's not going to change. What Dr. P. said is true."

"Please help us." I begged. "Make it such that he has no pain. Just let him go. Please."

The unreality struck me.

"My God," I said, awed, but hysterical with pain, "I, mother of Daniel, am actually sitting here and begging, absolutely begging for you to let my son die. How can I do that? How can this be?"

"It can be. Because Daniel's level is so very high."

"Please, will you help us? Will you turn off the ventilator, here, in the ICU, before he gets better or dies from something else?"

"I can't do that. Daniel would have to decide."

"You want a twenty-one-year-old boy to decide to die?"

"He has to request it himself. You cannot do it for him."

"But he doesn't know."

"Do you want me to tell him?" he asked. "Do you want me to tell him all the things that you know? That's the only way that he can make a decision."

I know all this, I thought. This is what I do for a living. Why is he telling me this?

Slowly I refocused. Because of Daniel, I remembered. Daniel must give informed consent. Daniel must make the request. Daniel, my baby. How can I do this? How can I let him be told all these awful things?

How? Because I love him. And, because I love him, I know that he must be given the choice.

"He's on medication," I said slowly, my voice sounding as though it was coming from outer space somewhere, far beyond the clouds. "His judgment is not good. He may not understand, or retain, what you tell him."

"I can stop his medications. Do you want me to do that?"

I looked at Leonard for confirmation. We both nodded. He held my hand.

"We can give him the information," Dr. B. said, from far, far away, in the distance, "but we cannot give him the choices. He must make any request himself."

"But he won't even know." I said, "He's only twenty-one. He doesn't know about these things. How will he know he has a choice?"

Dr. B. looked at me.

"You will have to give it to him," he answered.

18

To Tell the Truth

And so, on Monday, September 14, 1993, we decided to tell
Daniel the truth. The conditions were set by the physicians. Before Daniel was told, we were to meet with all of his
caregivers. Then, it would be decided who would go in to him
and tell him. The meeting was set for Tuesday afternoon. His
medication would be stopped immediately.

As Monday evening wore on, Daniel's pain and discomfort
increased gradually, until, finally, he demanded his medication.

"I want my medicine *now*!"

"Daniel, you can't have medicine tonight. I know that it
hurts, but you can't."

"Why not?"

Already, traces of the agony ahead overwhelmed me.

"Because," I said slowly and carefully, "the doctors want to
talk to you. They need you to have a clear mind and head."

"What about?," he asked, as I had known he would.

"About your condition."

I was sure he would say, "What about it?"

He didn't.

And his very silence told me volumes. He would not ask me.
He had to prepare himself for knowing.

All that long night, we looked forward to the tomorrow that
we knew would bring unbearable pain, and talked about other
things: the TV programs, his sisters and friends, home, and his

dogs. The hours passed slowly. We slept in fits and starts, and Daniel sometimes winced in pain.

But he never asked for medication.

The morning passed like all of the mornings before it. The nurses came in and out. The respirator techs adjusted his ventilator. Doctors came and went. Outside the door of Daniel's room, life in the ICU continued as always. The names of the patients on the board, with their nurses and physicians, were still there. Nurses sat at their computers. Stretchers and wheelchairs moved past us. Phones rang. The lights were bright and there were no shadows. From the dimness of Daniel's room, the ICU appeared like a stage and we, the audience, could watch in silence and detached fascination as life went on, and by. Actually, though I thought of it as we, Daniel could not watch the stage. His head could not be turned that far.

I stood by the head of Daniel's bed and leaned over to kiss him. As always, a hair brushed his face. As always, he complained. With his body so lacking in sensation, the touch of a hair on his face was agony. I withdrew and stood above him, trying to look at the world as he now saw it. Daniel's world.

Daniel's world had a TV in the top right-hand corner, suspended from the wall, always on. It had dim light from a window he could not see, and demanded always to be kept closed. Daniel's world could see the reflection of his monitors on the TV screen, if the picture was dim or dark. He could see the clock, plain square modern wood case, white face, with long thin Roman numerals. The face had a gold border around it. He could see the bulletin board to the right over the foot of the bed. It was almost empty. In contrast to his room at Strong, Daniel demanded firmly that no personal notes, items, or pictures, be placed within the narrow range of his vision. He refused his mail, and refused to have it hung where he could see it. There was only a clinical bareness, an emptiness, within his sight. It was as though Daniel had stripped all reminders of his past life away. He refused even to listen to his beloved music, most of the time. If he did allow music, it was something quiet and soothing and classical, and not his usual fare. And the player had to be kept out of his sight.

Were all reminders of his past life too painful to bear, I wondered? Or were they just not important, no longer relevant? All that was in Daniel's world was Daniel himself, his condition and the technology that supported his life.

When the appointed hour came, we gathered in a conference room in the ICU unit: his physicians, therapists, nurses, psychologists, and we, his parents. We reviewed his condition, his medical problems, past, present, future. I was asked to express my thoughts and, with a courage that came from somewhere I never knew existed, I repeated my request to the roomful of people: that Daniel be informed, and that choices be offered to him. Crying, I begged that he be spared this choice, and that we, his parents, be allowed to make it for him. I could not bear to consider the pain that knowledge of his condition, and the choices ahead, would give to my beloved child, my son, my baby.

But my request to spare him the pain was, once again, denied. Daniel was twenty-one. He was an adult. He was competent to make his own decision, and it had to be *his* decision. I bowed my head and acceded.

As the discussion of who, and how, continued, Daniel's nurse came to the door.

"Daniel wants you to know that he's ready," she said. "He says he knows what you are doing in here and he wants to hear for himself. He wants to know. He would like you to tell him right now."

Slowly, Dr. B. and Daniel's psychologist rose. Dr. P. remained sitting, and the rest of us all sat silently and waited for a few minutes. Unable to interrrupt, or hear, I finally got up and stood across the hall from Daniel's room. I could see Dr. B. talking, see the two bending over Daniel's bed.

After what seemed to me to be almost too short a time, they came out.

"He knows," Dr. B. said.

He knows, I thought, and fresh waves of pain washed over me. He knows all we tried to spare him. How can he stand knowing? But, what can he do about it, immobile and helpless? My maternal protectiveness screamed inside me, saying no, I should not have made them! How could I have made them tell him? How could I have caused him all the agony he must be feeling? And, beyond that, I knew that there was absolutely nothing I could do about it. Nothing that I could do to make the pain go away.

This is reality, I thought. My mind went back to my doctoral dissertation, about choices and human life. It went back to my sitting at the bedside of patients in pain, of dying patients. It went back to all of the neat and orderly thinking I had done on human beings and life and choices and self-determination. It sliced carefully and cleanly through my pain. This is reality, I said again to myself. And I have got to pull myself together and deal with it.

What is my ultimate responsibility, I thought, still leaning on the divider across the hall from Daniel's room? What is my responsibility, first of all, as Daniel's mother? And then, as a knowing and caring professional? And then, as a fellow human being? What is my responsbility?

I had begun a process. I had begun it out of the conviction that Daniel should not be *forced*, by circumstances, to live this agony, and that I, his mother, had as my ultimate maternal responsibility the care and protection of this child, still. I had assumed this responsibility when I had had him. Never, never in my wildest dreams could I have imagined that this thing that I now had to do would ever have been part of my maternal responsibility.

Mothers are to kiss scrapes away, I thought. And to comfort and reassure. To cheer on and encourage. To protect. How could being a mother encompass what I now had to do?

And then, I realized that it did.

. . . 19

The Hardest Choice to Offer

My husband and I walked into Daniel's room together. He sat in a chair in a corner, offering silent comfort. I walked up to the bed, the appointed choice-giver.

Sick, on a ventilator, with much of his hair out, bloated by edema, with tubes running from his body in every direction, I was still so *happy* to see Daniel. I loved him so much. I was happy to be with him and, for a moment, the happiness overwhelmed and wiped out my agony and terror over what I knew I had to do next. I basked in it. I smiled at him, held him. He smiled back, awkwardly. It was a moment of peace, the first of many in the too-few days that were to remain to us.

After a few minutes, I could feel myself internally pulling myself together, calling upon the greatest inner strength I ever had had to call upon. I felt odd. My skin tingled, and it seemed that I was not aware that I was breathing. The air around me seemed to be vibrating, somehow supporting and strengthening and energizing me. My eyes saw clearly, but saw only Daniel. Everything else in the room faded away to nothingness. I was ready.

And then, I faltered. I was terrified of not finding the right words, of not phrasing things right, of being clumsy and awkward and stumbling over the words, of what he would think. I was afraid of influencing him in any way. The doctors had been right, after all. It had to be Daniel's decision, and Daniel's alone.

Our job, as his parents, was to stand by, to help and support him in any decision he made.

How could I be sure, as his mother, that the choices I offered him would be clean and free of any of my own feelings? How could I be truly objective with my own child? I could not step out of my mother role. Could I really combine my mother self with my social-worker self and my philosophical self well enough to be all that I needed to be?

I looked down at Daniel in silence and he seemed to respect my need to think. He waited calmly.

I thought through my mother role. I wanted my child to be happy, to have the best possible that he could have. I wanted for him what any mother wants for her child. Only, Daniel, now, wasn't like just any other child. He was special. His needs were different. That was why we were all in this place, at this time. That meant that I had to be able to do things that were outside of the realm of what mothers usually do for their children. My goals were the same as those of any mother, anywhere. The ways open to meet those goals were different.

The way that was open, now, was the professional way. The way of considering Daniel as an autonomous individual, deserving of love, consideration, and respect. It was the way of using myself to the very best of my ability to offer Daniel the opportunities to determine the course of his own future, and of his own happiness. The best gift I could give my child, now, was my professional self, tempered with all of my love: my professional self to serve as his tool, to help him to understand and think through his situation, and to help and support the decisions that he made.

I could feel these three identities become one, a pulling together and an intense focussing on the goal before me: that of helping Daniel to determine his needs, and the conditions of his life.

Daniel seemed to sense that I was ready. He spoke first.

"They came in to tell me."

"What did they say?"

"You know. All that stuff. About how my level is very high and I won't be getting better."

"How did you feel about that?"

"Sucks."

"Did you know the things they told you already."

"No. Yeah. I don't know. Some of them."

"Dan, I broke a promise I made to you a long time ago. Back at Strong, I promised I would never have any secrets from you. I knew all this Sunday. And I didn't tell you."

"How come?"

"I just couldn't. I cried and cried and that's why I didn't stay with you Sunday night."

Silence.

"Will you forgive me?"

"Of course I will."

"Dan."

"What?"

"There's something else that I need to tell you. It's very important. I just want you to think about it. You don't have to give me an answer. Not now, not ever, if you don't want to. There's just another piece that you need to know."

"What?"

The silence seemed to stretch out into eternity, to that place where time and place stops and there is just stillness.

"Dan, there are choices that you have. At least two of them. And one of the choices has many other choices inside it. The other one doesn't have as many."

"What are they?"

"Well. You have the choice to live. To live and go through rehabilitation at Craig. You visited Craig and saw how it would be. You'd have a room to share, and they would teach you many things to help you to be as independent as possible. You could learn to use a sip and puff wheelchair, that you can operate by breathing. You could use a computer and control all kinds of stuff in your room with your eyes."

"You could have all the friends and music and TV and education and stuff you could want. You could live on your own in the community, or in a group home of some kind. You can hire and work with your own help. You can go out and do some traveling probably and other stuff I don't even know. You know we've talked about the Americans with Disabilities Act that was just passed. There will be all kinds of changes and new opportunities from that, too.

"Or, you can come and live at home with Dad and I and we will always give you everything that all of our love and our resources can give you. You know we've talked about how we can fix the house. You can do lots of things there on your own, and with us. We love you, and we would love you to be with us. You know that."

"I know, Mom."

"We would all have a lot to learn, but I know we can all do it together. Like we always do things."

"I know."

Silence.

"What's the other choice?"

"You have the right to refuse treatment. To ask that your vent be turned off. If you do that, you will die, because you know you can't breathe on your own." I smiled at him wryly. "Remember when you said you were ventilator dependent, at Strong, and I didn't believe you? Well, you were right. You are. And if you ask them to turn it off, you will die."

Daniel's eyes got big as saucers. They seemed to take up his whole face: large and so dark and round.

"But Mom, do they allow that? Is it allowed?"

"Yes, Daniel, it's allowed."

"Are you sure?"

"I'm sure."

"Well, then, I want it turned off."

"Dan, I think this is a really big decision. You need to think it through. You can't make it this quickly."

"I *have* thought it through. All these weeks. That's why all I do is watch TV. I want out."

"Dan, we have to go slowly with this. Tell me some of your thoughts."

"I don't want to live like this. I hate it. I have to depend on other people for everything. I have to wait for everything. I can't do anything for myself. I hate it and I want the vent off."

"What about friends?"

"I can't even talk to them. I can't go anywhere or do anything."

"What about the things you can do? That you'll be able to do once you're better? You're still very sick, you know."

Dan made a face.

"Like what?"

"Like going out. Going to shows. Spending time with us. Going to school."

"Forget it. I don't want to go to school like this. Don't you understand: I don't *want* to do anything like this. I don't want to live like this. I'll never want to do anything like this. All I'll ever do is take medicine and watch TV. That's not a life."

"I understand. I think you need to think about it more."

"All I've done is think about it. There's nothing more to think about."

"Don't make a final decision now. We'll talk about it more."

"All right. But I won't change my mind."

The silence filled the room. Neither of us spoke.

"You know, Mom, this is real hard to do. I wish I didn't have to do it."

"I know, Dan. I wish you didn't have to either. Dad and I tried to take the burden off you. They wouldn't let us. They said you had to decide. We didn't want you to suffer. But I think they were right."

Daniel nodded.

"What do I have to do?"

"When you've thought more, and if this is really what you want—God, Daniel, how can you? how can we? what are we going to do?—then you have to ask the doctors, yourself."

"Can't you?"

"No."

Silence.

"All right. I will."

"But Daniel, we must talk more. You have to be sure, very sure. Because once you're dead, you can't make any more choices."

"I know. But I am sure. I'll never change my mind."

"Just let's rest now, OK?"

"OK, Mom. Just sit here with me."

"Of course, Dan."

And after Daniel fell asleep, with no medications, I crept back to Leonard, who had listened.

"Did I do it right," I asked, shaking. "Did I say it right? Did I present it OK?"

Desperately, I needed reassurance that I had been fair in considering both options.

"You did fine," Leonard answered. "Daniel was lucky to have you."

"He won't have me much longer," I said, and, finally, the tears came. Silently, I cried from the depths of my being. I cried for Daniel's life, shortened and soon to be gone, by his own choice; for myself, and the loss of my child; for our family, never to be whole again, as it was even now, as long as Daniel was a part of it. I cried for all the might-have-beens, and all the never-were's. For his miscalculation with his dive, his strength which increased the force of the impact and the damage; the surgery consented to so quickly under so much pressure; the cardiac arrests that happened to so few; and the pacemaker insertion that closed off clearer diagnosis; the chest tubes that left holes; the hair that fell out; the medications I had tried so hard to refuse or amend; the respiratory distress syndrome that had sapped the vestiges of his meager reserves; and all of the other complications and problems that had occurred. It seemed to me that everything that could go wrong, had gone wrong in Daniel's case. There were no "lucky breaks," no last-minute reprieves. The world, which had always been beautiful, friendly, full of love and color and adventure, had become a desperate and unremittingly cruel place. I cried for my shattered dreams and illusions, and for Daniel's.

Daniel woke, and signaled to me.

I wiped my eyes, and went back to him.

And, for that evening, we watched TV, and spoke of other things, and pretended that this day had never happened, while each of us, alone inside, tried to grapple with it and to prepare ourselves, somehow, for what was to come.

. . . 20

Saying Goodbye

From the moment of our talk, I felt as though Daniel, and we, his parents, had somehow separated from the mainstream of humanity. The quotidian concerns which are the fabric of daily life no longer touched us. We had taken a turn onto an unpaved, but still smooth, small side road. I thought of Robert Frost's poem, "The Road Less Travelled By," and repeated the last words to myself:

> Two Roads diverged in a wood and I
> I took the one less travelled by
> And that has made all the difference.

I had always felt that, as a person, as a family, we had taken "the road less travelled by." Leonard and I had forged our own path, created our own values, with our children built the world in which we wanted to live. This was part of why, I thought, we were all as close as we were. As an individual, life circumstances and the choices I was given had placed me very much on a "road less travelled by." Sometimes, long before Daniel's accident, I would look over to the "main road" and wonder if I had done the right thing, if the way I chose as mine, the less travelled way, was really the best way for myself and those around me. Sometimes I even wondered if I was missing anything. The less travelled road, however, allowed me at times to join in with the mainstream, and, again and again, I reaffirmed that the path I had chosen was the right one for me.

This road, that Daniel had now chosen, this path upon which we followed him, did not allow for reaffirmation in the mainstream. It was too divergent.

The road had a pace, and a beauty, and a peace, all of its own which supported and sustained us, and somehow enabled us to live through the next two days. Time moved inexorably forward on this path, yet stood completely still. There were no rough edges, no bumps and rocks. It was all smooth and still. We played quiet music and listened to it together. We talked with our daughters who gave Daniel all the love and support they could, long distance, through us. They gave us support, calling almost hourly.

In Daniel's room, the machines whirred and hummed and clicked on, unaware. The dimness continued to pervade, merging with the sense of peacefullness. Nurses slipped in and out, quietly. Even the "stage" outside the room seemed quieter and more distant. We were in a small port, safe from any storms, as we slowly and lovingly helped Daniel to bring his ship gently to the other shore.

We discussed his decisions, and his plan. He spoke with his doctor, asked for the vent to be turned off, by himself, as the physicians had requested. Repeatedly, I begged them to ensure that there would be no pain, and they promised there would not.

I knew that Daniel suffered greatly from being unable to eat or drink, to taste anything. He sometimes watched me drink the tea they had for families in the ICU waiting room with so much longing it broke my heart, and I had tried never to drink it in front of him. I asked his doctor if, now that he had made this decision, he would allow him fluids. He agreed and I joyfully gave Daniel sips of of my mountain raspberry tea.

An amazing thing had happened. In giving Daniel the choice of life or death, I had given him back his life. He seemed to take much less pain medicine. He turned off the TV and was no longer in his drugged, withdrawn, stuporous state. He was alert and alive and responsible, and he knew it. It seemed to me that he was "in charge" of himself again, as he had been. I could feel the energy, the zest that seemed to emanate from him. He had things to think about, things to talk about, things to do, and the time was then to do them.

The peacefulness, and the isolation, made so many things possible as we began the last twenty-four hours. Daniel wanted to know about his funeral, his burial. We told him we would bury him in Boston, in the cemetery with his uncle and his grandfather and all the other Rothmans. We would purchase a family plot. We would, someday, all be together. He wanted a Jewish religious funeral, with no cremation. He asked about each family member who would share the cemetery with him.

In the evening, Daniel finished a tube feeding. Quietly, the nurse disconnected the tube. He was no longer receiving the nutrition that had sustained him during these brutal weeks. Medications were tapered and stopped. Still, the machines whirred on.

Daniel wanted a last strawberry daiquiri before he died. I laughed when he first told me. Why that? I asked him. He told me he enjoyed parties up at school, celebrations of summer at his fraternity house at which he had had strawberry daiquiris. We agreed. Leonard found a neighborhood store and brought back the ingredients.

"Not now. Not yet," Daniel said. "Not until tomorrow morning."

"We'll all make a toast," I agreed, "To you and to your future, and to the love we all share. To you until we are with you again."

"That will be good," Daniel agreed.

Later, he asked for a phone. He wanted to say goodbye to his friends, his grandmothers, his sisters. There were no phones for patients in the ICU, but this was important to him. I asked the nurse for a phone, and one was quickly provided.

Daniel could not, of course, speak on the telephone. It was my task to call the people he requested, to explain that Daniel was having his ventilator turned off, and that he wanted to say goodbye.

The agony of the people on the other end of the line touched me. They had not been through the process as we had. They were hearing this for the first time. There was a sharp intake of breath, a gasped "no," a fear of what to say, questions they were afraid to ask but needed to know, about the funeral. I calmly answered each one. Yes, Daniel had decided himself. He would be buried in Boston. The funeral would probably be Sunday. Yes, they could come. The funeral home was Levine Chapel. They had buried his grandfather, his uncle.

Daniel quietly listened to me answer, imagining the questions on the other end. Then, each time, I placed the phone by his ear. He quietly made his "nurse noise" to let the person know that he was there. Some said few words. Some talked for a long time. I do not know what they said.

And so, Daniel said a last, gentle goodbye to his fraternity brothers, his best friend from high school, his grandmothers, and his sisters. Only his sisters would call again. From the others, there would be the silence and respect for privacy that we needed.

I was unaware of the passage of time, but my exhaustion suddenly overwhelmed me. I wanted to stay, but I was so very tired. I had not lain down for such a very long time.

"What should I do, Dan?" I asked him. "I'm so tired. So tired."

"Stay with me, Mom. Please stay with me. It's the last night. You can rest later."

Tears came to my eyes. I stayed.

Though Daniel *said* it was the last night, it had not formally been agreed with his physicians. My mind leapt away from the finality. The last days, I could take in, and accept. The last night, seemed too enormous to contemplate.

But Daniel was calm, and sure.

"Sit by me, Mom, he said. I want to see your face all during the night. Can you just sit here?"

"Of course."

"I love you, Mom," he said, and, again, the tears came.

And so, we kept our vigil that last night. My husband dozed fitfully in the chair. I sat, at first rigid, in a high hard chair next to the bed. Daniel lay wide awake, and looked at me.

As the night wore on, despite my best efforts, my back began to hurt terribly. I could no longer sit perched high up on the office stool. Unable to sit, unable to move away from him, I finally took a pillow from under his hand, placed it on his body, and put my head down on it. Even in those last hours, my tired body dozed while Daniel watched over me.

Leonard was out of the room in the morning, and I was folding blankets in a corner, when Dr. P. came in. Daylight was barely appearing through the blinds in the darkened room. Dr. P. was a very early riser.

I could not know what Daniel was saying, since he made no sound. I could only hear Dr. P.'s responses.

"You want the ventilator turned off."

"OK."

"It is up to you to choose when and how."

"Today."

"This morning."

Silence.

"I have office hours until noon. I can come right after my office hours. A little after 12:00."

"OK."

He silently left the room.

Waves of shock and terror washed over me. Now it was no longer distant. It was here.

I walked up to the bed and turned to the clock on the wall. It looked just as it had always looked: brown plain case, gold border on the face, slim roman numerals. They hands pointed to seven A.M., exactly. There were five hours left.

I put my arms around Daniel.

"I heard what the doctor said," I said.

Silence.

"That's just five hours from now."

"I know."

"Are you sure, Daniel? Are you sure? Don't you want to wait? Just a little while. Just a few more days?".

I could feel myself starting to try to bargain with him. Anything, anything to delay the inevitable, this loss of my child.

"I'm sure. No more days. I've had enough."

"All right."

In a little time, Dr. B. came in to the room, and confirmed what Daniel had agreed with Dr. P. This was real, now, very real. He asked me if I wanted some medication for myself, to take the edge off and help me get through these next hours.

Daniel objected.

"I don't want you to have anything. You'll just go to sleep and I need you to be awake. No."

"But Daniel, I won't. This is so hard. I need something."

"No."

Yet, I slipped from the room for a moment, and took a small amount of medicine. I knew Daniel was wrong. I could never sleep through this.

Slowly, the hands of the clock moved forward. I could not take my eyes off it. I kept on going as usual, taking care of Daniel, suctioning his mouth, positioning his head, moving his arms around. Daniel wanted medicine this morning, and Dr. B. had ordered all that he wanted. Over and over, I asked the nurse for medicine. Still, despite his large doses, and my one small one, we were aware of every moment, alert, clear, calm.

Nurses and techs from neurotrauma came to say goodbye.

"Mom, do they know I'm going to die today?"

"I don't know Daniel. Maybe they do."

"How did they find out?"

"I don't know."

"It's nice of them to come to say goodbye."

Susan and Debbie called. They had wanted so much to be with them, but Daniel had refused. And we agreed. No need for them to have those memories. They were sad, but so supportive, and so loving. They talked and talked. They played him his favorite music. They played Debbie's tape of him, as a little boy, singing "The Burger Ate the Big Mac," "The French Frying Legion" and making silly noises. He had yelled his childhood names for himself onto the tape, too. He listened and smiled, over and over. They played him telling the story of "Little Red Riding Hood" as a little boy, the fractured fairy tale: "I'm gonna eat the grandma. I'm gonna eat the grandma, Of Riding Hoods I will not eat, there's nothing wrong with a grandma treat!" On and on. Over and over, he asked them to play the tape.

The technician came to turn off Daniel's pacemaker. Otherwise, it would keep his heart beating and prevent the peaceful death he wanted. It felt to me like death row: the final preparations, the little mechanical things that needed doing.

Again, I asked him, ashamed of my own weakness,

"Daniel are you sure?"

"I'm sure."

After a while, Daniel asked what I thought happened when you died.

"I don't know," I said. "We none of us can know. But I believe that there is a life of the soul that is immortal. It will be very different. I can't imagine it."

"That sounds OK."

"What will it be like to die?"

Again, I had to say I didn't know.

"But Daniel, you know. You almost died yourself, six times. Do you remember? It's like that, I think."

"I don't remember. Tell me."

"What you said was it felt like floating. It felt wonderful. You said you didn't ever want to come back and you were always diappointed when you woke up."

"So you think it will be good?"

"I think so, Daniel. But I don't know for sure. I know it will not be bad. It will be natural. Death is a part of life."

Daniel digested this in silence.

"What do you think about God, Dan?"

"I don't know. What do you think?"

"I think there is a universal intelligence that orders and har-monizes all things in this world. That is is above and beyond all that we know. That we can know very little of it until we die. You will know, soon."

"That sounds about right. I'll go with that."

And, again, we were quiet, each lost in thought.

When Daniel said it was time for the strawberry daiquiris, Leonard mixed them for us. We put them in plastic cups.

"To Daniel," we toasted. "To your life eternal."

"To Daniel."

"To our love. Together and united, always."

"To Daniel."

And all three of us drank.

And, all the while, the hands of the clock kept moving toward noon.

And then Dr. P. walked in the room. I looked out and saw our little support group gathered: Dr. B., the nurse, the psychologist who had been working with me, and Daniel's psychologist, the social worker. It was time.

I gathered myself together to face this last, final, step.

"We have to pray," Leonard said. "First we have to pray."

Dr. P. left us alone, and pulled the curtain.

I read Daniel his Bar Mitzvah portion, easily accessible since it was a regular part of the Shabbat service. I read him a selection from the readings, haphazardly, without time to really choose and reflect: "Happy is the Man." My voice shook and my hands shook and I could feel Daniel's attention focussed on me with complete intensity. We sang psalms, and Daniel joined in the singing. Last of all, we sang "Adon Olam"—Lord of the World. It seemed to me that I could hear Daniel's voice, singing the words. For the first time since our hurried goodbye before his surgery at Strong, I could hear his voice. It was strong, and familiar, happy and at peace.

It was the first time I heard it since July Fourth, and the last.

When we were ready, Leonard went to get Dr. P. As he walked in I kept my eyes on Daniel, smiled, always his mother, shielding him, this one last time, from the pain of knowing the moment was now. Dr. P. gave him sodium pentathol, an anesthetic, and his eyes closed, opened again. Quietly, peacefully, lovingly, Leonard and I each closed one. Daniel was asleep.

I leaned over and put my arms around him, hugging this child I loved with all my strength, strength enough to let him go, forever, from me. Leonard put his arms around me, and leaned over Daniel.

Dr. P. removed the ventilator from Daniel's throat, and walked out of the room, while I held on tightly.

And, gently, Daniel touched the other shore, and he was gone.

. . . Epilogue I

Our Lives Today

I sit by the window and write, as I have always done. The sun shines on the new spring grass, and squirrels run along the fence. The still-empty branches bulge with the promise of ...ing seems changed. On the open door of my room is a large black and white sticker Daniel got for me while I was studying for my Ph.D. in philosophy. It says "Question Reality."

It has been two-and-a-half years since Daniel has left us. They have been years of pain, years of sorrow, but also, incredibly, unexpectedly, years of growth. Losing a loved one changes you, forever. There is a sadness and a longing for the person I used to be, the one who trusted and believed that, if I loved my children, cared for them and nurtured them, they would grow up healthy and happy.

Those last days, I used to sing to Daniel "You Are the Wind beneath My Wings," and, in death, he remains as my inspiration, the source and goal of so much of my life. All of my strength, all of my growth, is drawn from his life and his courage.

Leonard and I left the hospital alone, hand in hand, the afternoon that Daniel left us. I felt so numb, so empty, that I had no sense of my own physical presence, or of what I was doing. We packed our few belongings, and an understanding airline agent booked us through to Boston, via Chicago. We would have to spend the night at O'Hare. We agreed—anything to be on our way.

We stood along the curb, with our luggage, like displaced persons, waiting for a cab that never came. Finally, a passerby noticed my tears, asked if she could help, and sent her son to take us to the airport. I spent the ride staring at the back of his head, trying to grasp the inescapable fact that I didn't have a son, anymore. In Chicago, Leonard lay on the floor and slept for a few hours, exhausted. I sat and stared at the rows of empty black seats. I could not think forward. I could not think backward. I could only be in the moment, alone, a mother who had just lost a child. When dawn came, finally, people arrived, and the airport filled with life. The crowds confused me, but I numbly followed Leonard onto the plane.

We buried Daniel on a sunny Sunday, in the cemetery that held his grandfather, uncle, and great-grandparents. We buried him a in large family plot which would eventually hold all of us together, once again. We scratched messages to him into the wood of his casket. I put some dirt from home into the hole, brought by a thoughtful friend, dirt from our front yard and from the place where Daniel, as a little boy, had dug a giant hole. He wanted to get to China, where all the dishes came from, and on the way, he was sure, he would find a dinosaur bone. Each of us, family and friends, gently lowered a shovelful of dirt over him, as we laid him to his final rest.

And then, still numb, we began to try to pick up the pieces, broken forever. We tried to build rituals for memories, to hold onto each other, to go on. As fall moved into winter, and the darkness and cold came, I retreated further and further into myself. Sometimes, it was all I could do to get dressed in the morning, and the walls of my house were the only things that held me up.

January 20 would have been Daniel's twenty-second birthday. From our icy deck, in the stillness of the early morning, we released balloons with messages of love for him, and sang happy birthday. One of my balloons became entangled in the bare branches of a tree. From the window, I stared at it and cried, for it seemed that everything always went wrong since Daniel died.

Sad and exhausted, I finally fell asleep. In a dream Daniel came to me, excited and pleased with his birthday balloons. He looked wonderful, healthy and strong. I explained about the balloon that was stuck. He said "Don't worry, Mom, I'll get the wind." Still dreaming, I felt a rush of cool air blow over me, and out of the window. When I awoke, the balloon was gone.

The story of the balloons has been special to me. The full version has been published in *Dream International*, a poetry journal, and is scheduled to be placed on the Internet. I also used the balloon idea to write a story for children who have lost a sibling. *A Birthday Present for Daniel*, beautifully illustrated by his best friend's mother, will be published soon, and hopefully will be of help to other families. Each year, we have repeated our little ritual, celebrating his twenty-third, and, recently, his twenty-fourth birthday.

Susan's pregnancy was difficult. Her blood count was in the danger zone over and over again, and we were warned about the threat of spontaneous hemorrhages. She was in and out of the hospital. The thought of the possibility of losing another child was too much for me to take in. I held it at arm's length, refusing to face it. Mercifully, toward the end of March, she gave birth to a healthy baby boy, named Daniel. Leonard performed the ritual circumcision himself, while I sat in the nursery and stared at the wood blocks, painted red, that spelled Daniel on the wall. And, in the months and years that have followed, this special blessing, this new Daniel, has warmed our hearts, and made us smile. This past November, after nine hospitalizations for her blood platelet disorder, Susan gave birth to another son, Sam.

In June of that first year, Debbie graduated from law school. She had gone from the funeral to the classroom, wanting to complete her work despite her sorrow. She struggled with a mind that could not think clearly, a memory that could not hold law, being too filled with her brother and her grief. She graduated the same day that Daniel would have graduated from the University of Rochester. Crying, I held baby Daniel tight and allowed some joy in my heart. My brave daughter had triumphed through the most difficult year of her life.

Passing through the anniversaries of that first year—the day of the accident, the week of decisionmaking, the moment of death, was agony, and, as the grayness of winter approached once again, the darkness closed in on me. This was never going to end, I thought, this miasma of sorrow and pain was going to go on and on all my life. I wasn't sure how long I wanted that life to be.

Then, Leonard lost part of his thumb in a circular saw accident, while building shelves. Complication followed complication, inexorably. Surgery, bone infection, more surgery, strong antibiotics left him weak and sick. In the recovery room, I stood in horror and watched another monitor—my husband's. Echoes of Daniel pounded in my head, and grew. Sleeping once again in hospital rooms, I fell quickly into the still-familiar, never-to-be-forgotten hospital routine, keeping my weary vigil as Leonard got sicker and sicker, and the doctors warned me that they were very "worried."

I went through the days in a haze of numbness. I had to get him out of the hospital, to take him home. I remembered how much I had wanted to take Daniel home, and how very impossible that had been. Finally, on Christmas day, I had my wish, and a weak and tired Leonard returned home in triumph.

On an emotional level, our marriage has been greatly affected by this tragedy in our lives. Very soon after Daniel's death, we were confronted with the sobering statistics that around 80 percent of marriages dissolve after the death of a child. Instead of turning to our spouse in our grief, we, like many couples, found that we grieved differently, and that each other was often the last person we could go to for solace. I grieved openly, talking of Daniel day and night, crying, unable to sleep. My ability to concentrate diminished frighteningly, and still today I forget simple things. I leaned on friends a great deal, became involved with other parents who had lost a child, spoke about Daniel and our decisions with anyone who was willing to listen. I read books about grief and healing, books that gave spiritual comfort.

Leonard buried himself in his work. He worked long hours, taking on more and more responsibilities. As chief of obstetrics and gynecology on a very busy service, this was easy to do. My grieving distressed him, and he became angry with Daniel, not just because of what he had done to himself, but because of what he had done to all of us. At the hospital he had constant reminders of his loss: young doctors, full of energy and excited about their work, emergencies and ambulances, patients on monitors. He could not get away from his pain, but he worked hard to suppress it. He could not talk about Daniel in public, except among close friends, and discouraged people who tried to comfort him.

Leonard felt I was letting Daniel destroy both of our lives, and that I did not care about him. I felt that he didn't care about Daniel as much as I did, because I saw little evidence of grieving. Knowing the odds were against us, we struggled to maintain lines of communication and connection. Finally one day, weary and frustrated by my constant tears, he shouted, "You know, I lost a child too, I hurt as much as you do."

This was a turning point in our relationship, and we have become closer and stronger with the passage of time. We are able to talk openly now, and to acknowledge our own feelings and each other's. We sense that we have passed the danger point, though we are still careful with each other's sorrows.

My relationship with my children has also changed a great deal. We all seem to have a tremendous need to be in touch, to be close. We cling together and give each other love and concern. We worry over little things which would never have troubled us in the past. We send each other gifts "from Daniel." But each of us grieves differently, too, and sometimes this creates stresses and problems. Susan's first reactions were similar to mine—tears and discussions, pictures and reminders everywhere. She became so upset that she eventually decided she had to put some things away, and think about Daniel and death a little less. I felt bereft, abandoned. She no longer expressed her grief as I did, and often closed off discussions. With the birth of her children and her full family and professional life, thoughts of Daniel necessarily became subject to the immediacy of her family's needs. Still, he is in her mind and heart and I know that she grieves for him every day.

From the beginning, Debbie rarely spoke about Daniel. She says the pain is too deep, and that her entire life has changed forever. She was the middle child, and is now the youngest. She and Daniel were both single, in contrast to Susan and I, and now she is single "alone." She feels that the family is changed forever and wishes the old days could come back. She does not light candles every month on the seventeenth, as Susan and I still do. Her grief is turned deeply inward.

In those early months, I was so concentrated on my grieving for Daniel that I paid little attention to my daughters. They were there to listen to me cry, but that was all I wanted or gave to them. After a few months, each in her own way, let me know that this hurt. It seemed that I didn't care about them any more, or, at least, cared less about them than about Daniel. As soon as I grasped this, my focus shifted. My girls were *alive*. They needed their mother, needed her for themselves and their lives and their concerns, and needed her to sort through some of their feelings about Daniel. Many times, I have set aside my grief to help them with theirs, stilled my tears to share their joys. They bring life and youth and hope to my heart, and I am grateful to have them, more grateful than I could have believed possible before the loss of Daniel. With Michael, Susan's husband, and Daniel and Sam, I can still draw a circle tightly around those dearest to me.

From the days of caring phone calls at the hospital, our friends have given us love, attention, understanding, and much time. They have stood beside us and held on to us, and are still giving us special love and support. In the first months, a different friend went out to lunch with me each day I was free. Each listened to the stories of Daniel that all parents who lose a child feel compelled to repeat, over and over. I did not go to parties or celebrations at all at first, and still rarely attend them, feeling out of tune with the mood of the event. We enjoy our friends one couple at a time, and appreciate the special thoughtfulness shared when it is a hard moment for us.

Sometimes I feel that our friends can never understand how I feel, and sometimes I am jealous and resentful. I recognized early that only someone else who had been through what I had been through could really understand me. In the first week of mourning, someone left a card on the table. It said "Compassionate Friends"—"for parents who have lost a child tragically," and gave a name and a telephone number. I posted it on the refrigerator door, where it remains still today. Alone, I went to my first meeting. I know that this kind of sharing does not help everyone, but, for me, Compassionate Friends was a place of love, understanding, and peace.

Over the months and years I have drawn strength and deep friendships from this source. I have taken all they had to offer, and now feel able to "give back," to help others as I have been helped. I run programs and facilitate groups. Though it is hard, I often work with the newly bereaved, and try to help them with sympathy, and with my lived experiences. Each month I go, leaving Leonard behind, spending am evening where my first and chosen identity is that of Daniel's mother. It is my relationship with him that gives life and meaning to this time.

One of the earliest and most important things I needed to do was to establish a memorial to Daniel. I wanted to ensure that his presence on Earth would survive, and that he would be remembered. I devoted much energy and effort to this project, and, during the first months of loss and desolation, I think that focussing on something so concrete was very helpful. From a desire for one memorial, several grew. Daniel's prep school, Severn School, established a memorial fund in his honor. To use the funds for something Daniel would have wanted, we donated an athletic scoreboard. Today, and every school day, the Daniel Rothman

Memorial Scoreboard looks down on happy students playing football, lacrosse, soccer, and field hockey. The scoreboard was dedicated in a beautiful ceremony and his number, thirty-two, was lit up throughout. Daniel also loved ceramics, and we were also able to donate a kiln to the school in his memory.

Our congregation named the religious school the Daniel Rothman Consolidated School, and a wonderful plaque in his honor attests to his values and ideals. When Daniel was little, we used to call him Dandelion, and at University of Rochester each spring, he enjoyed their annual Dandelion Day festivities. From another fund that had been established in his honor, we gave an annual "Dandelion Day"—a picnic for all the children in the religious school, with outdoor activities. Daniel would have liked them to have a day off from studies!

In Rochester, Daniel's fraternity brothers at Theta Chi planted a lovely memorial garden in his memory. It bears a plaque "In memory of our brother, Daniel Rothman." They also held a beautiful memorial service in his honor. At St. Mary's Hospital, where Daniel was working in the sleep disorder clinic at the time of his accident, an endowment fund in his memory was also established. In Rehoboth Beach, Daniel's favorite summer place, a memorial tree is planted in his memory, bearing his name.

It has been a labor of love to assist in establishing all of these memorials for Daniel. I think that they attest to the very special person that he was. I am honored that so many people have wanted to participate in these tributes to his life.

Today, we move more steadily on with our lives. Daniel is a part of everything we do, but we have had time to build some new memories, some good memories. Leonard's practice flourishes and I enjoy my teaching at Catholic University and my writing. Debbie practices law, and Susan teaches at an arts college. All of us in our own way, have found sources of strength-hand have used them to affirm both our loyalty to the past and our faith in the future.

These are the landmarks of our lives since we have lost Daniel. But his loss has affected every realm of our existence, and I believe it shall always do so.

I have stopped waiting to "heal." I accept that I shall always have this sorrow and this pain. I have tried to set myself to the task of integrating them into my being, of trying to make of his death something positive, leaving a legacy that will speak for him long after I, his mother, am gone. This book is a part of that legacy.

... Epilogue II

Echoes of Immortality

I have always believed that this world, this "reality" in which we human beings live, is a part of something greater, something vaster. I believe that, though we can never understand the totality, we all participate in it. If we are open to receive, we may have greater understanding and affirmation.

My explorations have taken me through many philosophical systems and religions, through mysticism and science. I have tried to walk upon the path of enlightenment while still unsure of its true meaning. While embracing no one system myself, I have tried to be open to all, and to take as much wisdom as I could from each.

I do not here want to share a particular religious belief or philosophy. I only wish to acknowledge that when we lose a loved one, the need to understand and to reach out becomes urgent, at times all-enveloping. We want to know that our loved one is at peace, is happy, or content, or any word you prefer to use. We want reassurance that our loved one "exists" somehow, somewhere. Our dearest wish is to communicate, to somehow establish a tie between our lives here today, and the lives of those we loved in the tomorrow that awaits us all.

Many times, I have shared my thoughts about this need with bereaved parents. Especially if the child was young, parents need to know that their child is taken care of, is comfortable, is safe. There are many paths to this kind of knowledge, and many of us walk more than one, sometimes in desperation, sometimes in joy.

I did not know how to begin my quest. I only knew that I had to open my mind and heart, and not presume that this affirmation would come from one particular source or another. I share my experiences to give faith that such special reassurances exist, somehow.

Two special moments came in dreams. One of my first was that of the birthday balloons. When my balloon had become stuck in the tree, rather than floating up to the sky with my secret message, I was devastated. My entire being was concentrated on Daniel, and on trying to reach him. Indeed, the whole idea of sending the balloon messages was focused on trying to communicate. When, exhausted from my emotions, I fell asleep, Daniel came into my dreams. I could practically touch him, and, for the first time, I could talk and receive an answer. I believe that Daniel's spirit sensed my need, and came to ease my sorrow.

Another dream came a few months later. Daniel came to me, accompanied by some other form that I could sense but not see clearly. There was instrumental music in the background.

"Sing me a song," Daniel asked me. "Sing me a special song about me. Just make it up."

"I can't, Daniel," I answered.

"Yes, you can. Listen to the music. Make a song to the music."

"But, Daniel, I can't just make up a song like that. The music will go on, and what if the words don't come? What if one line comes and then I can't think of the next one? I can't just write a song like that."

We argued back and forth until Daniel became impatient.

"Come on, Mom. Just do it. It will be all right. I'll take care of the music part. You just sing."

Very tentatively, I began to sing. Line after line came, in rhythm with the music. The poem wound its way through the music, staying perfectly in tune.

I was so amazed at this that I woke up. Unbelieving, and afraid I would forget, I ran to get paper and a pen to write the song. I wrote as fast as I could.

This was the song:

For Daniel

I sit in silent wonder
As the moon lights up the sky
Making patterns of the clouds
As they're slowly passing by.

> Making patterns so familiar
> I can almost feel and touch
> Of a child so strong and happy
> Of the boy I loved so much.

Of a child quietly sitting
Face touched by tall blades of grass
Looking down in silent wonder
As the insect armies pass.

> Of a cub scout quickly growing
> In his blue and gold all fine
> He can build his matchbox racer
> But never can stand still in line.

Of a schoolboy always laughing
With his jeans torn at the knees
Doing projects without number
In his 'boks and faded tees.

> Of a high school football player
> Proudly wearing 32
> Running down the fields of Severn
> Running hard as he could do.

Once again the patterns moving
As the boy becomes a man
Ever taller, ever broader
So mature, my college Dan.

> And the pattern ever changing
> Becomes fuzzy now, and dim
> Still I try, intently watching
> Try to find a trace of him.

And the teardrops fall unbidden
Each touched by the silver rays
As my son fades away from me
He has measured all his days.

Raindrops falling soft and gentle
Wash the patterns from the skies
I know somewhere they still linger
Beyond the vision of my eyes.

Still changing, ever growing
Keeping old along with new
Traces of the boy I carried
Traces of him as he grew.

In a pattern ever joyful
In a greater world than this
From the larger sky of heaven
I can still feel Daniel's kiss.

It has been accepted and published in various poetry journals. I have always enjoyed writing, but never sent anything to be considered for publication before. It was Daniel's spirit that gave me the courage, and the poem.

Another very special sign of his presence came through his memorial candles. On Yom Kippur, the Day of Atonement, it is the custom to light memorial candles to deceased loved ones. I particularly felt his presence as I lit the candle, comforting me in this most difficult act a parent must perform for a dead child. I lit the other candles: to my father, Leonard's father and brother, our grandparents. Memorial candles burn for twenty-four hours, more or less. One by one, the other candles went out, until only Daniel's remained. The wax didn't seem to be getting consumed. After three nights and two days, the candle finally extinguished itself. It had burned two and a half times longer than any of the others, two and a half times longer than it had been designed to burn. And, of course, three nights and two days can also been interpreted as thirty-two, Daniel's beloved football number.

On the second anniversary of his death, we made one of our four-times-yearly visits to Boston, to the cemetery. I brought a memorial candle to light. Again, I could feel his presence. Again, the candle stayed lit for three nights and two days. Again, the number thirty-two was with us.

Years ago, we had planted a little tulip garden, Daniel and I. I loved the color yellow, and had selected all yellow tulips for my garden. Daniel insisted on choosing one of another color, "to always remind you of me, every year." He chose a deep purple. Every year, when it was tulip time, Daniel's tulip bloomed, surrounded by a sea of yellow. I do not remember what happened the first year after his death, because I was too numb to notice. But on the second spring, I looked out, and there was his special tulip. I burst into tears remembering, and went outside to touch it. Though tulips never reproduce this way, and mine certainly never had, from out of the base of the stem of the Daniel tulip there grew a baby tulip. For me, this signified Daniel's tie to baby Daniel, and the unbroken line between them.

This past summer, on a family trip to Lake Tahoe, we went on a dinner cruise on a sternwheeler out into the lake. When we arrived, photographers posed us behind a white life preserver proudly inscribed "Dixie," the name of the boat. I painfully remembered another time, another trip, when we all posed behind a life preserver. It was one of our most wonderful trips, Daniel's favorite of all time, up the Mississippi on the Mississippi Queen. I wished with all my strength that Daniel could be here with us to share this day, this sunshine, this beauty. All during the cruise, I thought of him in sorrow. I reminded my family of that other trip, and the picture we still have. When the tour ended, we went to look at the pictures. One hundred photos were posted in little plastic "envelopes" on a wooden board. Each envelope had a number, so that people could easily identify and request their photo. We all stood in silent amazement, for our family photo was placed in envelope thirty-two. Daniel had been with us, after all.

There are just a few of the signs that I have been fortunate to receive. Each one is like a ray of sunshine. I know from other parents that many have received similar signs from their children. They bring faith, and comfort, and the love of our children to us.

They bring peace.

... Epilogue III

Philosophical Reflections

In the two-and-a-half years since Daniel's death, there have been times when I have had doubts about his decision, and about my role in it. There are times when I miss him so much that I would give anything to be able to touch him, no matter what his condition. There have been times when I wondered if the doctors could have made a mistake, if he could have improved. There have been times when I wondered if he would rather be alive, even as a C1 quadriplegic.

At those moments, I review again Daniel's condition, the reasons that we chose to give him choices, and the choice he made. I find reassurance in relating to the decision in a more reflective manner.

Before Daniel's accident, I had worked in long-term care for twenty years. A large part of my work involved assisting people to express their wishes regarding medication, treatment, and death. Another large part involved assisting people to consider and create advance directives for themselves. When the Patient Self-Determination Act was passed, an even greater emphasis was placed on patient rights, including the right to determine the conditions of one's own's death.

Perplexed in trying to understand my role, and my basis for assisting people with such decisions, I had returned to school and undertaken a doctoral degree in philosophy. I had chosen to do my dissertation on life-support decisionmaking in terminal illness. As I read and reflected, I arrived at two positions that seemed reasonable and right. Firstly, a concern for the dignity and self-respect of each human being, coupled with a belief in the ability of individuals to make reasoned and reflective choices, leads to an acceptance of the right of each person to make such choices regarding their own well-being. We call this autonomy. Secondly, an understanding that the desire of human existence must be individual happiness, self-realization, fulfilment, or some other similar term. The source, reason, methods, and goals of such self-realization must be determined by each autonomous individual. Autonomous individuals have values that direct and motivate their lives. These values give meaning to the life of each person, for meaning is drawn from values. To attain our goal of happiness, self-actualization, and fulfillment, we must be able to endow our lives with meaning. As we are each unique individuals, we each develop our values and meaning in our own way. We cannot impress our values and meanings upon another.

A life that is meaningful contains a variety of possibilities for action, goals, and direction, chosen by the individual. When we succeed in developing a life that includes these choices, we say that we have a good quality of life. When we are unable to actualize any of the things that give our lives meaning, we say we have a poor life quality.

Each of our lives constrain our complete freedom to make choices in a variety of ways. There are social constraints, such as laws, force, rules, and customs. There are psychological constraints, such as fears, mental limitations, mental illnesses. There are also physical constraints, such as age, weakness, and disability. Each person has a unique and individual combination of such contraints, some permanant, some transient. These constraints, in varying degrees, affect our quality-of-life by limiting our possibilities and choices.

Quality-of-life determinations are completely subjective, and we are limited in our ability to judge the life quality of anyone but ourselves. We can only view another's quality of life through the lens of our own beliefs, experiences, and values. The better we know someone, the more accurate we might be in assessing their quality-of-life. The better we understand our own subjectivity, the more we might be able to minimize its effects.

A good life, I think, flows, grows, evolves, moving always in the direction of self-actualization. We can achieve our goals best if we understand the things that give our lives meaning. We can use a variety of philosophical positions to describe a life of meaning but, in the end, we each can best develop our own.

Daniel's life was judged by him to be of good quality. Being a reflective person, he understood well the things that were meaningful to him. He loved physical action and activity, such as sports, the outdoors, building and construction. He took good care of his body to ensure that there were minimal constraints upon his physical activities with exercise, nutritional meals, and good hygiene. He was a very sociable person, and enjoyed his family, friends, and companions. He loved to "kick back" and talk about the meaning of life, the universe, religion, and other serious subjects, as well as sports, current events, and the way he saw his life. He loved to go to concerts, and follow the Grateful Dead, camping along roadsides and parking lots.

He was generous and kind, and concerned about others. He spent his freshman year in a dorm which required social action as a condition of residence. He visited nursing homes, worked in soup kitchens, and tutored younger children. He saw his life's work as helping others (along with having a good time for himself, of course). He was devoted to medicine, and looked forward to becoming a doctor. His job at the Rochester Sleep Disorder Center was, to him, his first step toward acquiring the knowledge he needed to pursue this goal. He learned everything he could, and was eager and willing to take on responsbilities.

Daniel loved to travel to other worlds and cultures, to camp in remote places, to explore new things. He lived life fully, and everyone that knew him described him as a "free spirit." He was often an inspiration to others, a motivator asking that everyone find, and pursue, their dreams. He loved challenges of all kinds, particularly physical challenges, and pushed himself to the utmost of his ability in all areas.

This was my son, until July 3, 1992.

These were his values, the things that gave his life meaning, his goals and aspirations.

I keep our last family photograph on the kitchen counter. We are all centered around his bed. We all are smiling, even Daniel. Only those present know the great effort the smile in the picture required. I keep it because his eyes look right at me and I feel that I can talk to him, smile at him. I keep it because each of us formed an unbreakable link in the circle that bound us together as a family, and I want to keep him included in that circle, still. Lastly, I keep it to remind me, in times of self-doubt and questioning, of how it really was.

Reality.

Daniel's head is cradled between two rolls of towels to keep it centered and straight. He cannot move it independently, and the towels keep it from rolling to one side. His thinning hair sticks to the side of his head. His face is puffy and swollen.

His tracheotomy tubing extends out from his neck, curls up the mattress and over the edge, connecting him to the respirator. Near his throat, a suction tube covered with soft plastic hangs over his chest. Every half hour at most, this tube must be thrust down his trachea, to clear out fluids. Daniel, brave as he is, winces in pain each and every time. There is no painless way to suction a person that frequently.

From his extended left arm, a network of IV tubing connects him to a bouquet of IV bags, each filled with a different medication, for a different purpose. On his extended right arm there is a blood pressure cuff. His chest, under the hospital gown, is puffy and bloated, giving him the appearance of a big rectangle with a small head on top. He "crackles" as you touch him, the trapped air bubbles under his skin popping and shifting. Under the gown, there are tubes deep in his chest, several of them. They work to drain the fluid from his lungs. The bag hangs by the side of the bed, a pinkish yellow. His catheter connects him to another bag.

His right leg, monstrously swollen and heavy from blood clots, rests on a pillow, the heel in a special protector. He lies on a special bed, puffy and filled with air, which automatically shifts his position to prevent bed sores. Above his head, the monitor records his vital signs. Next to his bed, a computer keeps records.

These problems are irreversible. He has Adult Respiratory Distress Syndrome, continual blood clots, unexplained fevers and infections, and open wounds that do not heal from his skin grafts. He has terrible headaches if his head is lifted the tiniest bit. In his weakened condition, he is prey to any infection, and any infection has the power to force him to a difficult and painful death, if his respiratory condition hasn't killed him first, or a blood clot to his lungs hasn't caused an excruciatingly agonizing death. His prognosis: death within three years, at most, from one or another of these causes.

What kind of life would be possible, for these three years? At best, he could be out of bed a few hours a day, in a wheelchair. At very best, he could operate the wheelchair with his eyes. He could watch TV. He might be able, with great effort, to do simple operations on a computer with his eyes, if he is able to sit up at an angle that enables this. He could communicate by mouthing words, and become angry and frustrated when they are not understood. He could never speak aloud, eat, or drink. These simple, basic pleasures would never be his. He would just exist, helpless, looking ahead to death and wondering when and in what form it would finally arrive.

Would he have any quality of life? Could he give such a life meaning? Would his values, goals, aspirations, be fulfillable in any way? When I ask myself these questions, I force my mind back, back to his life, his desires, his interests. Could he adapt to his condition, and find joy and pleasure? Though I believe that all human beings are adaptable, and that this is one of the factors that further inhibits subjective judgements of life quality, I do not think there was any possibility here. I think of Stephen Hawking, of other severely disabled people who paint with their mouths and use computers to do new and wondrous things.

I could not see any of these possibilities for Daniel. His disabilities were too severe. And, much as I loved him, I knew that he was no superlative genius who could devote himself to the next world-changing events.

Filled with mother-love and agony, I wanted to spare him pain, both physical and mental, and to decide for him to turn off his ventilator and let him go. My dedication to the principle of autonomy was swept away by the urgencies of the moment, until Daniel's doctors pulled me back, reminded me, and insisted. Only Daniel had the right to make such a decision about his life. If I believed the things I subscribed to, taught, lived by, could I deny him his basic human rights? My answer was no.

Having decided that Daniel had a right to know, I needed to ensure that he understood what was being said to him. Informed consent has several prerequisites: proper information must be given, in a comprehensible form; the patient must be capable of understanding, reasoning, and reflecting upon the information. There have to be options available, and the patient must be able to put these options into effect. Accordingly, I asked that his mind-altering medications be stopped, so that his reasoning and comprehension could be at their fullest. We spoke with his pulmonologist who agreed to abide by Daniel's decisions, and to remove the ventilator if Daniel made that request. I understood hospital policy: Daniel would be given information only. Choices had to come from himself and the family, so that the hospital and doctors could not be presumed to have influenced them.

And so, the information was given, the choices were made. Quality-of-life issues were considered in depth, and Daniel decision was indeed his own, and right for him. As his parents, we owed him no less that to assist him in his choice.

I do not want to be understood as believing that it is not possible to have a meaningful life under Daniel's conditions. I believe that it is possible, for others in other places and times. Daniel's decision was his own, made in his life circumstances, from his values and his understanding of the meaning of his life. I do believe, however, that, as human beings, we are each of us entitled to those choices.

I look back with pride and affirmation, with a strong belief that my son was true to himself until the end, and that his death was filled with love and dignity. As his mother, I can ask for no more.

. . . Postscript

From Daniel's Physician

Daniel's decision to discontinue his treatment with the ventilator was a very difficult one, not only for himself and his family, but also for the caregivers. On one hand, he was so young that it was difficult for the caregivers to let him go. On the other hand, his situation was one of repeated medical problems. Because of the problem with swallowing, removal of the tracheotomy tube was not an option. In a patient who could swallow, other methods of ventilation would be a possibility. These other methods would allow speech, and eating. Speech and eating were not a possibility in Daniel's case because of the severity of the neurological involvement. Therefore, the dilemma was to have Daniel choose to die, or to choose to go on without the basic human enjoyments of eating and communicating easily with other human beings.[1]

For me to remove Daniel from the ventilator was a painful thing to do. I had the choice of performing the act myself, delegating it to a respiratory therapist, or removing myself from

---

1. In Colorado, it is the law that patients have the right to choose to discontinue medical treatment. Although not as dramatic as with Daniel, other patients have chosen not to be resuscitated in the event of a cardiac arrest, that is, they chose in advance not to continue to be treated. Patients have also declined surgery for breast cancer, medication for emphysema, and for leukemia. They have decided that they did not want to be treated for their medical problem. In Daniel's case, the ventilator was a necessary treatment for him to stay alive. He chose to have that treatment discontinued. In Colorado, by law, the treating physician in such a circumstance is required to abide by the patient's directions. If the physician has a moral or ethical objection to abiding by the patient's direction, he or she is obligated to find another physician to care for the patient, and excuse him or herself from the care of the patient.

Daniel's care. I could not ask someone else to do what I was unwilling to do, nor could I desert Daniel at the time of his death. I have always felt that, along with the exhilaration of a successful end result in the practice of medicine, the territory also includes sticking by your patients in their rough times. In this situation, I felt that the only responsible course was to abide by Daniel's request, and remove the ventilator myself.

It is important that a time for the dying be established in this situation. The patient's needs should be respected, and all of the time needed should be allowed for saying goodbye. There should be no pressure of other work or responsibilities on the caregivers. This can best be done by mutual agreement by caregivers and patient.

I have faced a situation similar to Daniel's before. Many, many years ago, a patient with polio, ventilator dependent for many years, was discovered to have terminal metastatic pancreatic cancer. Once we determined that everything possible had been done, and that there was no possibility of a cure for him, he asked to be taken off the ventilator. As in Daniel's case, his entire family was informed, a time and date were set, and the ventilator was removed. I was younger and less experienced then: although we gave the patient a narcotic to ease the pain of dying, he was awake, and his death was agonizing for all—patient, family, and caregivers.

Because of this experience, I elected to give Daniel an anesthetic before disconnecting him from the ventilator. I didn't want him to suffer the sensation of suffocation when the ventilator was removed. That would have been unnecessary suffering for Daniel, and agonizing for his parents. I administered an injection of sodium pentothal to Daniel before removing his ventilator. This is the same medication that I have used perhaps a hundred times when I have needed to do something that was painful, such as a bronchoscopy or changing a tracheotomy tube. The injection was not lethal: patients receive this medication on a regular basis when they are going to have surgery. By giving Daniel this medication, he was enabled not to be awake for the event of dying. He could die peacefully of a natural cause (inability to breathe on his own), without further suffering.

As recorded by Juliet, my conversations to Daniel reflect a rather taciturn approach to him. This was deliberate. When such a momentous decision is being made by the patient it is not my place to insert my values into the discussion. My place is to give him facts, so that he can make his own decision. I have my own set of values, my own philosophy of life, but it was not my own life that was in question. Therefore, it was imperative that Daniel have all of his questions answered, and that he be aware of the alternatives. His decision was his, based on his set of values, his philosophy of life, and what was important to him.

There is one other issue to consider, and that is whether the patient is competent to make his own decision. In Daniel's case, he was alert and was not medicated when he made his decision. He also was not suffering from the acute depression that many people suffer when they suffer the devastating injury to the spinal cord which results in quadriplegia. I believe that he had been allowed the "cooling off period" necessary to make a rational decision, and that this was not the emotional decision one might make while still in a state of anger over one's situation.

I have had the occasion of being asked to discontinue a ventilator on yet another patient. He was very angry, very emotional, and, in my opinion, had not had this "cooling off period." I also felt that he had not had the "closure" in his life with his family that Daniel and the patient with the pancreatic cancer had had. Therefore, I felt that it was too early for him to decide to discontinue the ventilator, and that his decision was being made in the heat of the moment and not in a cool, rational environment. In that case, I excused myself from the case, as required by law, and another physician assumed the patient's care.

Juliet has done a marvelous bit of writing about the death of her son, Daniel. The issues she raises are very important, and need to be considered. They need to be considered with love and understanding, and this she has done very well.

—Peter Peterson, M.D.

Resources

Spinal Cord Injury

A. Organizations Providing Information and Services

National Rehabilitation Information Center
(800) 346-2742
Mailing Address:
8455 Colesville Road, Suite 935
Silver Spring, MD 20910

Library and information center on disability and rehabilitation. REHABDATA is a database of rehabilitation literature maintained by NARIC. It may be reached by telephone; FAX (301) 587-19647; or computer modem (ABLE INFORM to research REHABDATA). NARIC also provides brochures, factsheets, resource guides, and has a weekly newsletter. Also publishes the *NARIC Quarterly*, filled with resource information for living with spinal cord injury.

National Spinal Cord Injury Association
(800) 962-9629
Mailing Address:
545 Concord Avenue
Cambridge MA 02138

Largest information and referral resource for spinal cord injury in the United States. Bibliographical resources, information on quality care, efficient equipment and services, rehabilitation resources, etc. This private, non profit organization also supports locally based spinal cord injured groups for social, educational, and advocacy services. Quarterly magazine, *SCI Life,* covers research, lifestyle, legislation, and information.

Provides factsheets covering various areas of interest to SCI patients and families. Examples: Factsheet #1 explains spinal cord injury in detail; Factsheet #2 provides statistical information regarding the SCI population; Factsheet #4 addresses choosing a SCI rehabilitation program, provides a list of CARF (Commission on Accreditation of Rehabilitation Facilities) programs and NIDRR (National Institute of Disability and Rehabilitation Research) Model Spinal Cord Injury Systems programs. Factsheet #12 provides information on rehabilitation programs for ventilator-dependent SCI individuals.

Other helpful information available includes the *Pocket Guide to Federal Help for Individuals with Disabilities, Social Security Disability Claims,* and a *Publications Catalog.*

National Spinal Cord Injury Hotline
(800) 526-3456
Mailing Address:
2201 Argonne Drive
Baltimore, MD 21218

A 24-hour information and referral service.

Miami Project to Cure Paralysis
(800) STAND-UP
Mailing Address
1600 NW 10th Avenue #R-48
Miami, FL 33136

Multidisciplinary research program in spinal cord injury.

Paralyzed Veterans of America
(800) 424-8200
Mailing Address:
801 18th Street NW
Washington, DC 20006

Research, education, advocacy, and recreational programs for people with spinal cord injury, not limited to veterans. Legal information and questions about the Americans with Disabilities Act.

Spinal Network
(800) 543-4116

Publishes magazines and books on disability, especially spinal cord injury, and has resources and information.

B. Books and Other Literature

This selective list includes books and articles of interest to the spinal cord injury community. It is not intended to be a fully comprehensive list, but to provide a sampling of the literature.

Accent on Living. P.O. Box 700, Bloomington, IL 61702. Quarterly periodical.

Backman, Margaret. *The Psychology of the Physically Ill Patient: A Clinician's Guide.* New York: Plenum Press, 1989.

Burke, David. *Handbook of Spinal Cord Medicine.* New York: Raven, 1975.

Eareckson, Joni. *Joni.* Grand Rapids, Mich.: Zondervan, 1976.

Figley, Charles, and Hamilton McCubbin. *Stress and the Family, Volume II: Coping with Catastrophe.* New York: Brunner/Mazel Publishers, 1983.

Ford, Jack R., and Bridget Duckworth. *Physical Management of the Quadriplegic Patient.* Philadelphia: Davis F.A.Co., 1987.

Hastings Center. *Guidelines on the Termination of Life-Sustaining Treatment and Care of the Dying.* Bloomington: Indiana University Press, 1987.

Herek, George, Sandra Levy, Salvatore Maddi, Shelley Taylor, and Donald Wertlieb. *Psychological Aspects of Serious Illness.* Washington, D.C.: American Psychological Association, 1990.

Hochschuler, Stephen, Howard Cotler, and Richard Guyer. *Rehabilitation of the Spine: Science and Practice.* St. Louis: Mosby Year Book, 1993.

Journal of Neurotrauma. Dept. of Neurosurgery, New York University Medical Center, 550 1st Avenue, New York, 10016. This is a quarterly professional journal.

Kroll, Ken, and Erica Klein. *Enabling Romance.* New York: Harmony Books, 1992.

Levine, Stephen. *Who Dies? An Investigation of Conscious Living and Conscious Dying.* New York: Anchor Books, 1982.

Maddox, Sam, ed. *Spinal Network: The Total Resource for the Wheelchair Community.* Boulder, Colo.: Spinal Network, 1995.

————. *The Quest for Cure: Restoring Function after Spinal Cord Injury.* Washington, D.C.: Paralyzed Veterans of America, 1993.

Marinelli, Robert, and Arthur Dell Orto. *The Psychological and Social Impact of Physical Disability.* New York: Springer Publishing Co., 1980.

New Mobility, Miramar, 23815 Stuart Ranch Road, Malibu, Calif. 90265. Bimonthly periodical.

Nozer, Mark. *The Management of Persons with Spinal Cord Injury,* New York: Demos, 1988.

Phillips, L. et al. *Spinal Cord Injury: A Guide for Patient and Family.* New York: Raven Press, 1987.

Power, Paul, and Arthur Dell Orto. *Role of the Family in the Rehabilitation of the Physically Disabled.* Austin, Tex.: Pro-Ed, 1980.

SCI Life. National Spinal Cord Injury Assn. (800) 962-9629. A quarterly periodical.

Stingley, Darryl. *Happy to Be Alive.* Beaufort, S.C.: Beaufort Books, 1983.

Trieschmann, Roberta. *Spinal Cord Injuries: Psychological, Social, and Vocational Adjustment.* New York: Pergamon Press, 1980.

Whiteneck, Gale, et al. *Aging with Spinal Cord Injury.* New York: Demos Press, 1993.

————. *The Management of High Quadriplegia.* New York: Demos Press, 1989.

Zejdlik, Cynthia Perry. *The Management of Spinal Cord Injury.* 2nd edition. Boston: Jones and Bartlett, 1991.

$\mathscr{L}oss\ of\ a\ \mathscr{C}hild,\ \mathscr{G}rief,\ \mathscr{B}ereavement$

A. Organizations Providing Information and Services

A Place to Remember
deRuyter Nelson Publications, Inc.
1885 University Avenue, Suite 110
St. Paul, MN 55104

Special resources for infant death, books and special remembrances to help parents and family members.

Compassionate Friends (National)
P.O. Box 3696
Oak Brook, IL 60522-3696
(312) 990-0010

A self-help organization for parents, grandparents, and siblings. CF has a very extensive network of lcoal support grups offering programs, resources, and a library. Most CF groups meet monthly, and have telephone support as well. The organization also offers a quarterly national newsletter, a quarterly sibling newsletter, books to order, and yearly national and regional conferences.

Centering Corporation
1531 N. Saddle Creek Road
Omaha, NE 68104-5064

Centering Corporation also maintains a list of resources and books which are available through them.

Grief Recovery Help Line
(800) 445-4808
Hope for the Bereaved, Inc.
4500 Onondaga Street
Syracuse, NY 13219
(315) 475-4673

Carries books and resources on bereavement for adults and children, including information on how to form support groups. Also has support groups in the central New York State area.

National Catholic Ministry to the Bereaved (NCMB)
7835 Harvard Avenue
Cleveland OH 44105
(216) 441-2125

NCMB maintains a list of recommended resources, has a newsletter, *Journey*.

National Hospice Organization
1901 North Fort Meyer Drive
Arlington, VA 22209

National Sudden Infant Death Syndrome Alliance
10500 Little Patuxent Parkway, Suite 420
Columbia, MD 21044
(800) 221-SIDS (301) 964-8000

A national organization with a system of local support groups for parents who have lost a child through crib death. They will also provide information about SIDS.

Parents of Murdered Children, Inc.
100 E. 8th Street
Cincinnati, Ohio 45202
(513) 721-5683

The national organization has a network of local support groups for parents and families. They also have a traveling Murder Wall, which carries tributes to murdered loved ones; SOS, which helps families who feel that they still have unresolved legal issues; and Parole Block, which helps to keep murderers in prison.

Pen-Grandparents
P.O. Box 3304
Jasper, AL 35502
(205) 384-3053

A correspondence network for bereaved grandparents.

Rainbow Connection
477 Hannah Branch Road
Burnsville, NC 28714
(704) 675-5909

"Helping people grow through loss, grief, and change." Maintains a list of books and resources which can be ordered through Rainbow Connection.

Rothman–Cole Center for Grief Recovery & Sibling Loss
4513 N. Ashland Ave.
Chicago, IL 60640-5401

SHARE
St. Elizabeth's Hospital
211 S. Third Street
Belleville, IL 62222
(618) 234-2415

SHARE assists in the establishment of community support groups for parents whose baby has died due to miscarriage, ectopic pregnancy, stillbirth, or newborn death. Maintains educational materials and resources and provides referrals to local groups.

Suicide Hot Line (National)
(800) 333-4444

Survivors of Suicide, National Office
Suicide Prevention Center, Inc.
184 Salem Avenue
Dayton, OH
(513) 223-9096

A network of support groups for those who have lost a loved one through suicide. Your local hospice and hospital are good sources of information on support group networks, services, and bereavement resources in your area.

B. Books and Articles

The following list of books and articles have been found to be especially helpful by the members of the Anne Arundel County (MD) chapter of Compassionate Friends. It is not meant to be an exclusive or comprehensive list, or to espouse a particular viewpoint or theory about life and death.

Anderson, George. *We Don't Die*. New York: Berkeley Books, 1989.

———. *We Are not Forgotten*. New York: Berkeley Books, 1992.

Bereavement, A Magazine of Hope and Healing. Bereavement Publishing, 350 Gradle Drive, Carmel, IN 46032. Nine issues yearly.

Berezin, Nancy. *After a Loss in Pregnancy*. New York: Simon and Schuster, 1982.

Brooks, Ann. *Grieving Time: A Year's Account of Recovery from Loss*. New York: Dial, 1985.

Cook, Alician Skinner, and Daniel Dworkin. *Helping the Bereaved: Therapeutic Intervention for Children, Adolescents, and Adults*. New York: Basic Books, 1992.

Davis, Deborah. *Empty Cradle, Broken Heart*. Golden, Colo.: Fulcrum, 1991.

Eadie, Betty J. *Embraced by the Light*. New York: Bantam Books, 1994.

Fitzgerald, Helen. *Grieving Child: A Parent's Guide*. Hamden, Conn.: Fireside, 1992.

Grollman, Eric. *Talking about Death: A Dialogue Between Parent and Child*. Boston: Beacon Press, 1976.

———. *Explaining Death to Children*. Boston: Beacon, 1967.

———. *Living When a Loved One Has Died*. Boston: Beacon, 1977.

———. *Straight Talk about Death for Teenagers: How to Cope with Losing Someone You Love*. Bsoton: Beacon, 1993

Grootman, Marilyn E. *When a Friend Dies: A Book for Teens About Grieving and Healing*. Minneapolis: Free Spirit, 1994.

Hewett, John. *After Suicide*. Louisville, Ky.: Westminster Press, 1980.

Knapp, John. *Beyond Endurance: When a Child Dies*. New York: Schocken Books, 1986.

Kübler-Ross, Elisabeth. *On Children and Death*. New York: Collier, 1983.

———. *On Death and Dying*. New York: Simon and Schuster, 1970.

Kushner, Harold. *When Bad Things Happen to Good People*. New York: Schocken, 1989.

Levine, Stephen. *Healing into Life and Death*. New York: Anchor Books, 1987.

Livingston, Gordon. *Only Spring: On Mourning the Death of My Son*. San Francisco: Harper San Francisco, 1995.

Lord, Janice Harris. *No Time for Goodbyes: Coping with Grief, Anger and Injustice after a Tragic Death*. Ventura, Calif.: Pathfinder, 1987.

Martin, Joel, and Patricia Romanowski. *Our Children Forever*. New York: Berkeley, 1994.

Moody, Raymond. *Life after Life*. New York: Bantam, 1976.

———. *The Light Beyond*. New York: Bantam, 1989.

Moore, Thomas. *Care of the Soul*. New York: Harper Perennial, 1994.

Morgan, Earnest. *Dealing Creatively with Death*. Burnsville, N.C.: Celo, 1988.

Morse, Melvin. *Closer to the Light*. New York: Ivy Books, 1990.

Peck, Scott. *The Road Less Traveled*. New York: Simon and Schuster, Inc., 1978.

Schiff, Harriet Sarnoff. *The Bereaved Parent*. New York: Penguin Books, 1977.

———. *Living Through Mourning*. New York: Penguin Books, 1986.

Stevens, Velma. *Grief Work*. Nashville, Tenn.: Broadman Press, 1990.

Tengbom, Mildred. *Helping the Bereaved Parent*. St. Louis: Concordia, 1981.

Ulene, Art. *How to Survive the Death of a Loved One*. New York: Random House, 1987.

Williams, John, and Frank Cherry. *The Grief Recovery Handbook*. New York: Harper Perennial, 1988.

For Children

Buscaglia, Leo. *The Fall of Freddie the Leaf.* Thorofare, N.J.: Slack, Inc., 1982.

Mellonie, Bryan, and Robert Ingpen. *Lifetimes.* New York: Bantam Books, 1989.

Nystrom, Carolyn. *Emma Says Goodbye.* Elgin, Ill.: Lion Publishing, 1990.

Powell, E. Sandy. *Geranium Morning.* Minneapolis: CarolRhoda Books, 1990.

Rothman, Juliet. *A Birthday Present for Daniel.* Amherst, N.Y.: Prometheus Publishers, forthcoming.

Advance Directives and Patient Rights

The following list is a sampling of national organizations and resources which provide information to the public on advance directives and patient rights.

American Association of Retired Persons
Legal Counsel for the Elderly, Projects Section
601 E Street N.W.
Washington, DC 20049
(202) 434-2120

Planning for Incapacity: A Self-Help Guide is a series of state-specific guides. Thirty-one states, plus the District of Columbia, were available as of March 1993. Cost: $5.00 per guide; $3.00 if more than one is purchased.

American Bar Association Commission on
Legal Problems of the Elderly
1800 M Street, N.W.
Washington, DC 20036
(202) 331-2297

Health Care Powers of Attorney: An Introduction and Model Form, is a public education booklet which provides background information about healthcare decision making, a sample health care power of attorney/living will form, and instructions for use. Cost: $3.50 prepaid. May be ordered in bulk: 11–99 copies, $2.50 each; 100–499 copies, $1.50 each; 500 or more copies, $.75 each.

American Hospital Association
840 Lake Shore Drive
Chicago, IL 60611
(312) 464-4613

The AHA has produced "Put it in Writing" (#169908 and 3169909) guides to advance directives, and also a video for consumer education.

American Medical Association
515 N. StateStreet
Chicago, IL 60610
(800) 621-8335
(312) 464-5000

Guide to Living Wills and Powers of Attorney for Health Care is available free of charge. There are two versions: one for patients, one for physicians. Both provide general information.

American Society of Law and Medicine
765 Commonwealth Avenue
Boston, MA 02215
(617) 262-4990

Information for professionals and consumers available on request.

Baylor College of Medicine: Center for Ethics,
Medicine, and Public Issues
1200 Morrison Street
Houston, TX 77030
(713) 798-5290

Provides education and consultation on individual care issues.

Boston University School of Public Health:
Law, Medicine and Ethics Program
80 E. Concord Street
Boston, MA 02118
(617) 638-4626

Information regarding health care proxies and living wills.

Center for Bioethics
University of Toronto
88 College Street
Toronto, Ontario M5G 1L4
(416) 978-2709

Living Will, by Peter Singer, is a simpler variation of *The Medical Directive* (see below). Cost: $5.00. Bulk: 10–49, $4.00 each; 50–99, #3.00 each; 100 or more, $2.00 each.

Choice in Dying
250 W. 57th Street
New York, NY 10107
(212) 246-6973

Choice in Dying has general and state-by-state information and forms for healthcare powers of attorney and living wills. Single copies for specific states may be requested free of charge. Also has videos, factsheets, and provides information and counseling for families in legal disputes.

Hastings Center
255 Elm Road
Briarcliff Manor, NY 10510
(914) 762-8500

Hastings Center is a general resource for bioethics issues and advance directives. Publishes *Hastings Center Report,* a monthly journal of bioethics with many relevant articles regarding laws, specific issues, and opinions by professional bioethicists.

Kennedy Institute of Ethics, Georgetown University
37th and P Street, N.W.
Washington, DC 20057
(202) 687-8099

Research information on advance directives available. Publishes a bioethics journal and has extensive library and resource information regarding advance directives.

National Health Lawyers Association
1620 Eye Street, N.W.
Washington, DC 20006
(202) 833-1100

Patient Self-Determination Directory and Resource Catalog, available free of charge, provides information and resources regarding advance directives and patient rights and advocacy. This excellent, thorough guide contains statutory requirements, organizational listings, practical considerations, frequently asked questions, and other information.

University of New Mexico School of Law
Center for Health Law and Ethics, Institute of Public Law
1117 Stanford Street N.E.
Albuquerque, NM 87131
(505) 277-5006

The *Values History Form* by Joan Gibson can be used as a valuable tool to clarify issues and assist individuals and designated powers of attorney in making healthcare decisions.

General Internal Medicine Unit   *Harvard Health Publications*
Massachussetts General Hospital   164 Longwood Avenue
32 Fruit Street   Boston, MA 02115
Boston, MA 02114
(for single copies)   (for multiple copies)

The Medical Directive, by Linda L. Emanuel, M.D. and Ezekiel J. Emanuel, M.D. includes six illness scenarios, and allows the individual to consider interventions and goals of medical care desired for each. Bulk: 50–99 copies, $1.00 each; 100–499, $.75 each; over 500, $.50 each.

Advance Directive forms, laws, and policies differ from state to state. To be sure that your directive is effective for your state, or to receive guidelines specific to your state, you may contact your State Attorney General's Office, State Medical Society, State Bar Association, State Hospital Association, State Office on Aging, or your local hospital.